What is Islam?

By

Jamaal Zarabozo

1435 H - 2014 G

Preface

In the name of Allah, Most Compassionate, Most Merciful. All praises are due to Allah; we praise Him; we seek His help; we seek His forgiveness; and we seek His guidance. We seek refuge in Allah from the evil in our souls and the badness of our deeds. For whomever Allah guides, there is none to lead him astray. And for whomever He allows to go astray, there is none to guide him. I bear witness that there is none worthy of worship except Allah, for whom there is no partner. And I bear witness that Muhammad is His servant and Messenger.

I would like to take this opportunity to express praise and to thank Allah for giving me the opportunity to write an important work of this nature. May Allah forgive me for my shortcomings in presenting His religion.

I would also like to express my heartfelt thanks to the noble Shaikh Muhammad al-Turki of the Ministry of Islamic Affairs, Endowments, Da'wah and Guidance for his support. I would also like to express my thanks to Ahmad Ba-Rasheed for his continual efforts as well.

There are many people that I would like to thank for their help in this particular work. First, I must express my thanks to my beloved wife who is always a source of assistance and help. Special thanks must also go to Dr. Abdulkarim al-Saeed, Br. Nahar al-Rashid, Dr. Mohammad al-Osimi, Dr. Ahmad al-Teraiqi and Br. Jalaal Abdullah. I can only pray that Allah rewards them and blesses them in both this life and the Hereafter.

I pray that Allah accepts this work from me as being solely for His sake. As with all such work, the responsibility for any mistakes lies with the author. I ask Allah to forgive me for my shortcomings and to guide me to the Straight Path.

Jamaal Zarabozo
Boulder, CO
Oct. 14, 2005

Introduction
The Goal and Motivation for Writing this Book

This is a very important time for the publishing of clear and concise material about Islam. Today, Islam is often pictured in a very unflattering manner in many parts of the world—not much different than it was in the not-so-distant past. A Western author writing about the life of Muhammad (peace and blessings of Allah be upon him) wrote,

> When the war blazed up between Islam and Christianity, lasting for ages, animosity grew severe between the two sides; and each side misunderstood the other one. It should be admitted, however, that the basic misunderstanding was more on the part of the westerners than the easterners. In fact, immediately after such violent intellectual disputes — in which argumentative debaters overloaded Islam with vices, degradation and abasement without taking the trouble to study it — mercenary writers and paid-poets set out to attack the Arabs, but their attack was a merely false, contradictory accusation.[1]

---

[1] Quoted from Afif A. Tabbarah, *The Spirit of Islam: Doctrine & Teachings* Hasan T. Shoucair, trans. (2nd Edition revised by Rohi Baalbaki, 1988, no other publication information given), p. 9. For an in-depth study by a non-Muslim of how Islam has been portrayed in the Western literature, see Norman Daniel, *Islam and the West: The Making of an Image* (Oxford, England: Oneworld Publications, 1993), *passim.* Another important work is Minou Reeves, *Muhammad in Europe: A Thousand Years of Western Myth-Making* (Washington Square, New York: New York University Press, 2000), *passim.* It is interesting to note her explanation of why Westerners attempted to attack the person of the Prophet *per se.* She writes on p. x, "The trouble started with early medieval Christian polemicists. They chose not to attack Islamic theology, which was too seductive in its simplicity and clarity, and which raised too many awkward questions about Christian dogma. Nor could they cast doubt on the pious practice of ordinary Muslims. Instead, anticipating the worst excesses of tabloid journalism, they personalized the issue and attacked the Prophet of Islam, dispensing with all but the barest knowledge of any facts and

There is no need to go into details but today such misunderstandings concerning Islam have continued from all sorts, including some public and church leaders in the West.

Unfortunately, since many of the masses are unfamiliar with Islam beyond what they see in the mass media—which of course recently has been filled with a terrorist taint—it is not surprising that such misrepresentations of Islam resonate with the public as a whole.[1] The easiest and probably the most productive cure for this situation is by reaching out to those people and allowing them to hear what Islam is truly all about. One must go beyond the hype and get to the true authentic teachings of the religion. (Unfortunately, it is also a sad state of affairs that today one must also go beyond the picture that the Muslims themselves give non-Muslims of Islam. Although, in general, Christianity or Judaism is not blamed for the misdeeds of Christians or Jews, today Islam is still often blamed for the misdeeds of Muslims, even when the practices of such Muslims clearly violate the tenets of Islam.[2])

Unfortunately, today the negative views and misrepresentations of Islam are not simply an issue of one's personal religious beliefs. The ramifications have gone far beyond that and touch upon the security and politics of the world as a whole. Most harmful though is that as Islam is misunderstood and continually painted as the "other" and a source of evil, many are closed off to its beauty and its priceless truths that it has to offer to humankind. In reality, in these troubled times, there is a great need to turn to the guidance from God, which is exactly what Islam is all about.

---

inventing falsehoods. Muslims could not reply in kind, since they are told by the Qur'an to revere Jesus as a holy prophet."

[1] An interesting discussion of how Islam is dealt with in one Western country's media is John E. Richardson, *(Mis)Representing Islam: The racism and rhetoric of British broadcast newspapers* (Amsterdam: John Benjamins Publishing Company, 2004), *passim.*

[2] For a Muslim to set a bad example of Islam is grave indeed. Allah has even taught the Muslims to make the following supplication: "Our Lord! Make us not a trial for the disbelievers, and forgive us, Our Lord! Verily, You, only You are the All-Mighty, the All-Wise" (60:5).

The goal here is not to deal with the misinformation that is being spread about Islam. The goal here is simply to present what Islam truly is, based on the original and universally recognized sources of Islam: The Quran—or, in other words, the book revealed from Allah (God) to the Prophet Muhammad (peace and blessings of Allah be upon him)—as well as the words and guidance of the Prophet himself.[1]

The Intended Audience for This Work

The person targeted by this work is anyone who is interested in a basic introduction to the fundamental beliefs and practices of the Islamic faith. An attempt has been made to be as concise as possible—but with the hope that the reader will be encouraged to study Islam in more depth. For the purpose of more in-depth study, many other important books will be recommended or referred to in the footnotes.

It should also be noted that this book is written by a "Western" convert to Islam and it is assumed, since it is written in English, that a good number of its readers will be either of the West or familiar with the West. Thus, many of the references will be related to issues with which the people of the West would be most familiar and with which the author is also most familiar.[2]

The Place of this work among the other introductory works

There is a plethora of books introducing Islam to non-Muslims. Especially since 9/11, one can enter virtually any major bookstore in the United States, for example, and find numerous

---

[1] The example and actions of the Prophet (peace and blessings of Allah be upon him) are known as his *sunnah* while his statements are termed *hadith*. Upon reading further about Islam, one will come across these terms quite often. For the sake of familiarity, "example" and "statements" of the Prophet will be used throughout this work. Also note that these reports about the Prophet (peace and blessings of Allah be upon him) are usually referenced by stating the source work in which they are found. This traditional manner of referencing is followed in this work.

[2] Hence, there will be very little, if any, reference to Eastern religions or philosophies. This author has, however, studied those subjects and some of his findings may be found in Jamaal al-Din Zarabozo, *Purification of the Soul: Concept, Process and Means* (Denver, CO: Al-Basheer Publications and Translations, 2002), pp. 11-20.

introductory texts. Obviously, some of them are quite decent.[1] Many of these are written by non-Muslims, some no doubt sincere in their wish to faithfully present the religion of the Muslims. As a Muslim, this author can state that, for the most part, these authors have a tendency to miss the true spirit of Islam and what Islam is all about. These works have a tendency to concentrate on secondary issues, historical developments among the Muslims themselves or deviations from the original Islam, leaving the reader ignorant of the essential spirit and teachings of Islam.[2]

On the other hand, many Muslim writers writing for Western audiences take a very apologetic or modernist approach to Islam. One cannot write a book introducing others to Islam while, at the same time, twisting or distorting the true meaning of Islam as believed in by millions of people, as opposed to the individual version held by the author of such a book. Similarly, one cannot write an introductory book about Islam while trying to present a new "version" of Islam. The responsibility of the one who wants to present Islam to others is to present it as it truly is, honestly and frankly, without

---

[1] Some of the more detailed works and some of the better quality works written by Muslims themselves do not, for various reasons, make their way onto the shelves of the major bookstore chains. However, they may still be found via major internet outlets or bookstores specializing in Islamic works. Some such works will be mentioned in the next section of this introduction.

[2] Two examples may be given here. Two of the most popular "textbooks" on Islam are: Frederick Denny, *An Introduction to Islam* (New York: Macmillan Publishing Company 1994) and John Esposito, *Islam: The Straight Path* (New York: Oxford University Press, 1998). Although neither of these two authors can be classified as antagonistic to Islam, they still fail to highlight and truly present the essence and beauty of Islam. Denny's work has 17 chapters and almost 400 pages. Of those, only about five to six chapters (about 100 pages) touch upon what could be considered the core issues of what Islam is all about. The rest deal with civilizations in Egypt and Mesopotamia, the history of Judaism and Christianity, later developments of Sufism, "modern reform movements" and the like. Esposito has six chapters and less than half of his work touches upon central issues. The rest is mostly concerned with political or historical developments. One could read either of these two books without knowing much about what Islam is truly all about and what is the great attraction of Islam to so many millions around the world. (Note both of these works have just come out in new editions but nothing in them changes the content of the above comment.)

trying to hide or change anything. It is the Muslim's belief that this is Allah's religion. Hence, one must present Allah's religion as it has been revealed to and propagated by the Prophet Muhammad (peace and blessings of Allah be upon him) himself. The presentation must be honest and candid, leaving the reader to decide for himself—based on sound knowledge—if he wishes to pursue this religion further or not.

The sources and methodology for this book

Any reliable book on Islam must be founded upon the Quran[1] and the statements and guidance of the Prophet Muhammad (peace and blessings of Allah be upon him). Although the original Arabic texts of both the Quran and the Prophet's sayings are available, one has to resort to modest translations to convey their meanings to non-Arabic speakers. With respect to the Quran, two translations can be recommended and will be used throughout this work. They are *The Noble Quran: English Translation of the Meanings and Commentary*, translated by al-Hilali and Khan[2], and *The Quran: Arabic Text with Corresponding English Meaning*, translated by "Saheeh International."[3] These two are recommended due to their translations being based upon the understanding of the Quran as can be traced back to the Prophet himself and his closest Companions.

As for collections of the statements and actions of the Prophet (peace and blessings of Allah be upon him), two important collections are available in complete form in English. They are known as *Sahih al-Bukhari*[4] and *Sahih Muslim*.[1]

---

[1] The reader should note how the verses of the Quran are referred to: *soorah* or "chapter" number followed by verse number, e.g., 2:16 would mean the sixteenth verse of the second chapter.

[2] Muhammad al-Hilali and Muhammad Muhsin Khan, trans., *The Noble Quran: English Translation of the Meanings and Commentary* (Madinah, Saudi Arabia: King Fahd Complex for the Printing of the Holy Quran, n.d.). This translation has also been published by others and is easily available over the internet.

[3] Saheeh International, *The Quran: Arabic Text with Corresponding English Meaning* (London: AbulQasim Publishing House, 1997).

[4] Muhammad Muhsin Khan,trans., *Sahih al-Bukhari* (Riyadh,Saudi Arabia:Darussalam Publishers and Distributors, 1997). Available via many sources on the Internet.

There are also a number of secondary works that are extremely helpful in understanding the religion of Islam.[2] Some of the most important of them, which also form sources for this work, are:

Commentary on the Creed of at-Tahawi by ibn Abi al-Izz.[3] This is a very important classical work that expounds on the details of the Islamic creed.

Umar al-Ashqar's "Islamic Creed Series," including *Belief in Allah in the Light of the Quran and Sunnah* and *The Messengers and the Messages in the Light of the Quran and Sunnah.*[4]

Bilal Philips' *The Fundamentals of* Tawheed *(Islamic Monotheism).*[5]

Afif A. Tabbarah's *The Spirit of Islam: Doctrine & Teachings.*[6]

As for the "methodology" that the author has followed herein, what is presented is based, to the best of this author's ability, on the teachings of the *ahl al-Sunnah wa al-Jamaah,* this is the community of Muslims who trace their beliefs and teachings directly back to the Prophet (peace and blessings of Allah be upon him) himself. No attempt has been made here to try to "reinterpret" what

---

[1] Abdul Hamid Siddiqi, trans., *Sahih Muslim* (Lahore, Pakistan: Sh. Muhammad Ashraf Publishers & Booksellers, n.d.). Also widely available.

[2] The ones mentioned in this introduction are of a general nature. More specialized works will be referred to throughout this work. Note also that this author benefited as well from two of his earlier works: *He Came to Teach You Your Religion* and *Purification of the Soul.*

[3] *Commentary on the Creed of at-Tahawi by ibn Abi al-Izz* (Muhammad Abdul-Haqq Ansari, trans., Riyadh: Ministry of Higher Education, 2000).

[4] These are part of a series of about ten books that touch upon all of the basics of Islamic beliefs. They are published by International Islamic Publishing House, Riyadh, Saudi Arabia.

[5] Bilal Philips, *The Fundamentals of* Tawheed *(Islamic Monotheism).* (Birmingham, United Kingdom: Al-Hidaayah Publishing and Distribution, No date given).

[6] Translated by Hasan Shoucair and revised by Rohi Baalbaki. Although it is an excellent introductory text on Islam, unfortunately, the edition available to this author has no publication information.

has been accepted as truth by the Muslims for centuries and which continues to be the dominant view of approaching Islam today.

Before proceeding, one should note the usage of the words Allah and God. Allah is the "personal name" of God, much like Yahweh (later interpreted as Jehovah). Thus, Allah and God can and will be used interchangeably.

The Belief in God (Allah)

In reality, belief in Allah is the cornerstone of the entire faith of Islam. All of the other Islamic beliefs and all Islamic practices revolve around the proper belief in God. For this reason, perhaps more than any other religious community in the world, the belief about God in Islam has been delineated in great detail. In fact, a famous Muslim scholar, ibn Abi al-Izz al-Hanafi, once stated that it can be concluded that all of the verses of the Quran, in one way or another, touch upon the belief in God.[1]

Thus, any earnest discussion of the religion of Islam has to begin with the concept of the belief in God. Indeed, it must be a detailed discussion of this topic for, again, everything else in Islam is firmly grounded in and based on this fundamental belief. In fact, according to Islamic teachings, it is the belief in One God alone, with no partners, that all prophets taught and which was the core message of all of their messages.[2] It is the first step, the most important step and an invaluable step in the process of understanding one's own reality.

How Can One Know About God?

Before presenting the Islamic view on this question, a history of some current paradigms will be given.

Beginning in the first half of the 17th century in Christendom, as the disconnect between "scientific fact" and

---

[1] He concluded this by showing that all of the Quran, in essence: (1) Discusses Allah's names, attributes and actions, and this is part of knowing what to believe about Allah; (2) Calls people to Allah's worship alone, without ascribing any partners to Him and leaving everything that is worshipped other than Him, and this is related to the actions unfolding from belief in Allah; (3) Commands, forbids and requires obedience to Him, and this is all part of the rights or implications of the belief in God; (4) States how Allah honors those who believe properly in Him, how He treats them in this world and what He honors them with in the Hereafter; all of this is the reward for proper belief in God; (5) Discusses those who have associated partners with Allah and whom He has punished in this life or would punish in the next, this is the just reward of those who abandon the proper belief in God and acting upon that proper belief. See Ibn Abi al-Izz, *Commentary on the Creed of at-Tahawi by ibn Abi al-Izz*, p. 13

[2] This shall be discussed in more detail later.

"Biblical truths" grew greater and greater, philosophers Edward Herbert, Voltaire and a number of American leaders such as Thomas Paine, adhered to a philosophy known as deism. These philosophers believed in God, the Creator and in morality. They believed in what they called "natural religion" that could be discovered through the use of reason. Hence, they downplayed the role of revelation and the teachings of the church.

A number of factors led to the development of this philosophy. Key among these factors was the fact that, as shall be discussed later, these scholars could not deny the rational proofs behind the existence of the Creator. Hence, they had to begin with that premise. However, due to their disappointment with what was being taught by the Church, they were driven to the conclusion that the truths of this world are known through human reasoning and are not in need of any type of revelation from God. Indeed, there was no need for God to send any further information behind what could be derived by humans themselves. Beyond that, they also argued that God had no further role to play in this creation. Thus, they looked upon God almost like a watchmaker who, after having created the watch and wound it up, would then just sit back and allow the watch to work on its own without any interference from the watchmaker.

In sum, according to this view, humankind has been left alone by the Creator—alone to find its own way of how to behave and live in this great creation. Perhaps without reference to its philosophical roots, this has become the way of life of many of the world's inhabitants today. They do not see any need to turn to God to know how they are supposed to live their lives in this world. Indeed, as a political philosophy—known as secularism—this is the dominant philosophy in the world today.[1] (As shall be discussed later, this view

---

[1] As is so often the case, ideologies or philosophies have developed in certain areas of the world due to particular circumstances of that area and then they are developed into universal ideologies. For example, the rift between scientific fact and church teachings was something prevalent in Christendom but has never been a problem—to this day—within the Islamic world. Hence, the arguments that supported those philosophers in their attitude towards God's revelation were completely restricted to the revelation that they were

actually contradicts one of the attributes of God: that He is merciful and compassionate to His servants, that humankind should not think that they have been left without guidance and that there is no purpose directly related to God in their creation.)

The Islamic religion does not deny that humans have been endowed with great reasoning power and natural instincts. Many scientists—including those philosophers referred to above—could not deny the various signs that point to the existence of the Creator. Hence, they wholeheartedly accepted the notion of the existence of God. In the history of humankind, this notion has not been a problematic issue. In fact, the Quran states the matter in this way, quoting the words of earlier messengers: "What! Can there be a doubt about Allah, the Creator of the heavens and the earth?" (14:10). Their problem lay in their not knowing about God properly and not having access to a true and preserved revelation from God. This highlights the importance of recognizing the proper way to know about God.

Islam recognizes that God has created the human with an innate ability to recognize and understand the truth that he has a Creator and a God. In fact, the Prophet Muhammad (peace and blessings of Allah be upon him) himself said, "Every child is born on the *fitrah* (the natural way, the religion of Islam)."[1] In other words, every child is born with the inclination and leaning toward the truth and the ability to recognize the reality of the existence of God.

The basic concept about God, therefore, is known to everyone —philosopher, thinker and layman alike. At the same time, no gracious and mature human should be willing to completely ignore and turn his back on the very foundation of his creation. There should

---

familiar with, the Bible. Their arguments fall apart once the revelation—such as the Quran—is completely consistent with the true scientific facts of the physical world surrounding the human. Perhaps—and, of course, only God can know this—if those philosophers would have been exposed to the Quran as God's revelation instead of the Bible and the teachings of the Christian Church, they may have come to some very different conclusions concerning the revelation from God.

[1] Recorded by al-Bukhari and Muslim.

be, then, a desire within the soul of every human to know his Lord and Creator, the one who has blessed him with his very existence.This should be an innate and automatic feeling within the soul of every human.

However, there is another important point that needs to be made about God, the Creator.God, obviously, is a distinct and separate being from His creation. Hence, God is not something within the realm of human experience, human thought or human testing. In fact, the way to know about God is not by philosophizing in a quiet room or remote part of the world—that can point one to the irrefutable fact of His existence and greatness. But to know the details about God and, in particular, to know what one's relationship with God should be, one can only turn to God Himself and to His revelation. There is no other possible way.

The revelation from God as embodied in the Quran and the inspired words of the Prophet Muhammad (peace and blessings of Allah be upon him) have thus presented a clear and unequivocal presentation concerning God. It removes all doubts about His existence, His omnipotence and His omniscience. It also answers all the questions surrounding how one should behave toward the Almighty. In addition to that, by God's mercy, He has provided extensive information about Himself, through His names and attributes, such that He does truly become the beloved, the soul object of worship and the main inspiration for one's life.

In the following pages, there shall be a summary of the magnificent teachings about God as found in Islam. It cannot be claimed that this summary is anything more than the tip of the iceberg compared to the vast amount of information that is conveyed about God in the Quran and Sunnah.

The Belief that God is the Sole Creator and Sustainer of all Creation

There is one thing that definitively stands out when one reads the Quran: Allah instructs humankind to ponder over the creation with all its subtleties and magnificence. At no time do the teachings of the Quran shy away from reflection and rational thought. Indeed, these foundations of knowledge have been invoked over and over in the Quran as a path that will lead to only one conclusion: That there is no way that this creation as one can witness and appreciate it today could have possibly come into being except through the intent and creation of a great, divine and masterful creator.[1]

In fact, in one verse, Allah has given a powerful argument that was convincing to humankind for hundreds of years: "Were they created by nothing, or were they themselves the creators? Or did they create the heavens and the earth? Nay, but they have no firm belief" (52:35-36). This has been clear to many, many people: They obviously did not come here by means of nothing nor did they create themselves. Hence, they are the result of the act of a Creator—a Creator who is in himself self-subsistent and not himself a created being.

Although this belief is innate and clear, doubts and misconceptions repeatedly come to humans from all sorts of different

---

[1] The classic saying even among the Bedouin Arabs was, "Camel dung indicates the presence of a camel and footsteps indicate that someone has walked." It is said of one of the early Islamic scholars, Abu Hanifah, that a group of the people who had entertained some doubts about God came to him to discuss the unity of the Creator and the Lord. He said to them, "Before we enter into a discussion on this question, tell me what you think of a boat in the Euphrates which goes to shore, loads itself with food and other things, then returns, anchors and unloads all by itself without anyone sailing or controlling it?" They said, "That is impossible; it could never happen." Thereupon he said to them, "If that is impossible with respect to a ship, how is it possible for this whole world with all its vastness to move by itself?" This story has also been narrated from people other than Abu Hanifah. Cf., *Commentary on the Creed of at-Tahawi*, p. 9. Umar al-Ashqar provides another example: "A few years ago, the sands in the Rub' al-Khaali' desert (the Empty Quarter) were blown away by a windstorm to reveal the ruins of a city that had been covered by the sands. Scientists began to examine the contents of the city to try to determine the period in which it had been built. Nobody among the archaeologists or others even suggested that this city could have appeared as a result of the natural actions of the wind, rain, heat and cold, and not by the actions of man. If anyone had suggested such a thing, people would have regarded him as crazy and would have taken pity on him." Umar al-Ashqar, *Belief in Allah in the Light of the Quran and Sunnah* (Riyadh: International Islamic Publishing House, 2000), p. 125.

sources.[1] In different eras, different forms of confusion may come to people. Today many people are confused over the question of creationism and evolution. In fact, some even argue that "creationism" is not sound science while "evolution" is.

Currently, a popular explanation for the existence of the cosmos is the big bang theory. In fact, the *Microsoft Encarta* refers to it as the "currently accepted explanation of the beginning of the universe."[2] It is quite good of them to refer to it in that manner because "science" keeps changing its "facts" and explanations. It is exactly as Allah has described in the above-quoted verse, "Nay, but they have no firm belief" (52:36). Those who have turned away from God have to admit that they do not truly know what they believe and tomorrow their belief may be completely different from what it is today because, in reality, it is not built upon something firm.

It seems though that the dispute between the big bang theory and creationism is more hype than it is substance. The big bang theory, as the *Encarta* explains, "proposes that the universe was once extremely compact, dense, and hot. Some original event, a cosmic explosion called the big bang, occurred about 10 billion to 20 billion years ago, and the universe has since been expanding and cooling."[3] But this begs the question of who created the matter that was involved in that big-bang?[4] If that matter still requires a creator, is there any proof that the same creator did not create new types of creatures later in this cosmos?

Of course, there is a much bigger problem in relation to the big bang theory: How could such a random explosion lead to the

---

[1] It would be politically incorrect today to call these "ungodly," "evil" or "Satanic" sources. However, in the end, this conclusion will be unavoidable as these forces are attempting to take humans away from what is right and true to some other forms of belief.

[2] © 1993-2003 Microsoft Corporation. All rights reserved.

[3] © 1993-2003 Microsoft Corporation. All rights reserved.

[4] Note that even if there is some evidence of a cosmic big bang many years ago, this step as a possible act done by God in the process of forming this cosmos does not necessarily contradict Islamic beliefs. The exact manner in all steps and details by which God created the different parts of this cosmos is not known and, at best, one can only put forth theories.

consistency, excellence and beauty that one sees in this universe? What, for example, was the beauty and organized cosmos that was set into motion after Nagasaki and Hiroshima were bombed?

Amazingly, atheists and materialists still refuse to see what is obvious to their very souls and make statements that are ludicrous to say the least. For example, the famed atheist Huxley once actually stated, "If six monkeys sat at typewriters and banged on the keys for billions of years, it is not unlikely that in the last pages they wrote we would find one of the sonnets of Shakespeare. This is the case with the universe that exists now. It came about as the result of random forces which played with matter for billions of years."[1] Waheed Uddeen Khan, using "materialistic" kind of reasoning has replied to such a statement quite well: "Mathematics, which has given us the concept of probability, itself states that it is mathematically impossible for this universe to have come into existence by accident."[2]

In addition to the realization that this existence must have had a creator, one can also notice the equilibrium and balance that exists throughout the universe. The order is so precise that it is sometimes referred to as "the delicate balance of nature." It is truly amazing how everything works together—even within one's own body. Without such cooperation between the different organs of the body, for example, there would be no possibility of continual life. This observed phenomenon leads to a number of other important conclusions.

First, the order and cooperation between the various inanimate elements of the universe—which have not been trained or taught—is a sign that they are still under the control and regulation of the creator. The different objects of this creation have no power, ability or goal of their own, as otherwise they would most likely go against the universal laws and order. They have only what has been granted to them by the overall Creator and Master of all of the

---

[1] Quoted by al-Ashqar, *Belief in Allah*, p. 131.
[2] Quoted by al-Ashqar, *Belief in Allah*, p. 131.

different component parts of the universe. Their level of inter-working and cooperation is such that it points to their being all under the authority of one Being, who must have both full knowledge and complete power to sustain and guide them. If this were not the case, only chaos could be rationally expected, especially given the large number of atoms and other particles that make up everything that is in the universe.

Second, there is a clear sign that the Creator and Master of the Universe is one and only one—there cannot possibly be more than one Creator of this balanced and unified cosmos. This follows from the previous point. If there were more than one creator, each having a will and power, then it would not be expected that the cosmos would have the unity, balance and equilibrium that it currently exhibits. This is known as "the argument of exclusion" and is an issue that has been discussed by philosophers in detail in the past. For example, in *The Commentary on the Creed of at-Tahawi*, one can find,

> This argument [of exclusion] runs like this: If there were two creators and they disagreed about something, such as one wanted to move X whereas the other did not want it to be moved, or one liked to make Y a living being whereas the other liked to make it lifeless, then, logically speaking, there are only three possibilities. First, the wills of the two are both carried out; second, only the will of one of them is carried out; third, the will of neither of them is carried out. The first case is not possible because it requires the existence of contraries. The third possibility is also ruled out because it would imply that a body is neither moving nor not moving and this is impossible. This would also imply that both of them are incapable of carrying out their wills, which would disqualify them for being God. Finally, if the will of one is realized and not of the other, he alone will deserve to be God and the one

whose will is not realized could not be considered God.[1]

Thus, the premise that there is only one original and unique Creator, Sustainer and Ultimate Power over this universe is something that is both innate in humans and concluded easily and logically. In fact, it can be said that Islamic scholars are so convinced of the obvious truth of this point that, according to the famed Islamic scholar ibn Uthaimeen, all of mankind except the most arrogant and haughty accepts and recognizes this aspect of monotheism, namely, that there is no Lord and Creator but the One Lord and Creator.[2] This is so because this belief is ingrained in the nature of humankind. Humankind recognizes and realizes that this creation must have had a Creator. Humankind also realizes that this Creator must only be One.[3]

Although in the previous paragraphs there was something of a digression into other topics that are of interest today, one can summarize the Islamic view on Allah being the sole Creator and Sustainer of the creation by allowing the Quran to speak for itself and express the essential truths:

"Certainly, Allah has power over all things" (2:20).

"He is the Originator of the heavens and the earth. How can He have children when He has no consort? He created all things and He is the All-Knower of everything. Such is Allah, your Lord! None has the right to be worshipped but He, the Creator of all things. So worship Him (Alone), and He is the Guardian over all things. No vision can encompass Him, but His Grasp is over all vision. He is the

---

[1] *Commentary on the Creed of at-Tahawi*, p. 4.

[2] Muhammad ibn Uthaimin, *Sharh Usool al-Imaan* (Fairfax, VA: Institute of Islamic and Arabic Sciences in America, 1410 A.H.), p. 19.

[3] In addition, Christians also distinguish between God the Father—the Creator—and "the Son." With very rare exceptions, most of them will not say that "the Son" created the Universe. This author also knows from many ex-Hindus who became Muslim that most Hindus also have a concept of one and only one unique creator above all of the gods that they believe in.

Most Subtle and Courteous, Well-Acquainted with all things" (6:101-103).

"Do they seek other than the religion of Allah, while to Him submitted all creatures in the heavens and the earth, willingly or unwillingly. And to Him shall they all be returned" (3:23).

"And unto Allah (Alone) falls in prostration whoever is in the heavens and the earth, willingly or unwillingly, and so do their shadows in the mornings and in the afternoons" (13:15).

Once that it is concluded that Allah is the only Creator and Sustainer of the universe, many corollaries fall into place. In addition, perhaps the most important question a person can ask himself is: What should be one's relationship with that one creator? This leads directly into the next topic of Allah being the only one worthy and deserving of worship.

The Belief that Allah Must Be the Only Object of Worship

It is of extreme importance to realize that recognizing the facts about the existence of only one Creator and Sustainer is not all there is when it comes to the Islamic concept of "belief in God." Actually, recognizing that fact is something that should be beyond question and should be clear to all as, again, it is something innate in human souls. The far more important and subtle issue is what one then does concerning one's belief in only one Creator and Sustainer. Actually, once one understands and accepts the attributes and qualities of Allah as discussed in the previous section, the relationship that one should have with the Creator and Sustainer becomes clear. In other words, the conclusion should flow from the unquestionable premise.

Perhaps a couple of examples will make this point clearer. As noted above, in reality, Allah is the only perfect and great being in existence. He is the source of all goodness and help, as He alone has power over all things. He is active in His creation and He has not left it to run its own course without His ever-existing acts of creating and re-creating.

Furthermore, Allah is perfect and great, far above all human comprehension and imagination. In general, what is a person's attitude toward that which they find to be perfect, great and marvelous? It is usually one of awe, respect and honor. Furthermore, can one treat any other being as equal to or even be held in comparison with the Creator? On this point, God says, "Do they attribute as partners to Allah those who created nothing but they themselves are created?" (7:191). God also says, "Can the One who creates and the one who cannot create be equal? Don't you learn the lesson?" (16:17).

In addition, though, Allah is the source of all of one's bounties and blessings. Indeed, He is the source of one's life and everything that has been prepared in this creation for him. Thus, Allah says in the Quran, "If you count the Blessings of Allah, never will you be able to count them" (14:34). Can humans actually bring about these bounties for themselves without the aid and help of Allah? Allah gives another example when He says, "Say (to the disbelievers), 'Tell me, if Allah took away your hearing and your sight, and sealed up your hearts, who is there –a god other than Allah—who could restore them to you?' See how variously We explain the lessons, yet they turn aside" (6:46).[1] Even the most precious of life's commodities, rainwater, still cannot be produced unless Allah creates the clouds with the appropriate characteristics to produce rain. In a beautiful passage in the Quran, Allah reminds humans of this important bounty as well as many others when He says,

> Say (O Muhammad), "Praise and thanks be to Allah, and peace be on His slaves whom He has chosen (for His Message)! Is Allah better, or (all) that you ascribe as partners (to Him)?" Is not He (better than your gods, He) Who created the heavens and the earth, and sends down for you water (rain) from the sky, whereby We cause to

---

[1] The same procedures today that can partially restore eyesight in some humans fails in other humans, even when all of the other conditions seemed similar. In fact, doctors always speak about percentages or success rates because ultimately the result lies in a power much greater than the mere material means that God has put at their disposal.

grow wonderful gardens full of beauty and delight? It is not in your ability to cause the growth of their trees. Is there any god with Allah? Nay, but they are a people who ascribe equals (to Him)! Is not He (better than your gods, He) Who has made the earth as a fixed abode, and has placed rivers in its midst, and has placed firm mountains therein, and has set a barrier between the two seas (of salt and sweet water). Is there any god with Allah? Nay, but most of them know not. Is not He (better than your gods) Who responds to the distressed one, when he calls Him, and Who removes the evil, and makes you inheritors of the earth, generations after generations. Is there any god with Allah? Little is that you remember! Is not He (better than your false gods, He) Who guides you in the darkness of the land and the sea, and Who sends the winds as heralds of glad tidings, going before His Mercy[1]? Is there any god with Allah? High Exalted be Allah above all that they associate as partners (to Him)! Is not He (better than your so-called gods, He) Who originates creation, and shall thereafter repeat it, and Who provides for you from heaven and earth? Is there any god with Allah? Say, "Bring forth your proofs, if you are truthful" (27:59-64).

Is it logically admissible for one then to hold an attitude of disrespect, neglect and arrogance towards the One and Only God? Indeed, can the attitude toward that One great and marvelous being who bestowed such bounties be anything but humility, humbleness, gratefulness, love and devotion?

These two examples, of Allah's solitary power and ability and of Allah's solitarily bestowing of bounties, should be sufficient to demonstrate the point that Allah alone has the right to be loved,

---

[1] "His Mercy" here is a reference to rain.

honored and worshipped. This is a point that Allah makes numerous times in the Quran in various ways, speaking to those who recognize that there could be only one creator and yet at the same time they ignore Him and worship false gods and false objects of worship. Thus, for example, Allah says, "Say [to the polytheists, O Muhammad], 'Whose is the earth and whosoever is therein? If you know!' They will say, 'It is Allah's!' Say [then to them], 'Will you not then receive admonition?'" (23:84-85). Again, Allah says, "Say [to the polytheists, O Muhammad], 'In Whose Hand is the sovereignty of everything? And He protects (all), while against Whom there is no protector, if you know.' They will say: "(All that is) Allah's.' Say [then to them], 'How then are you deceived and turn away from the truth?'" (23:88-89).

In fact, it is Allah alone who can offer guidance. The false objects of worship cannot do this in the least. Thus, Allah says, "Say: 'Is there of your (so-called) partners one that guides to the truth?' Say: 'It is Allah Who guides to the truth. Is then He, Who gives guidance to the truth, more worthy to be followed, or he who finds not guidance (himself) unless he is guided? Then, what is the matter with you? How judge you?' And most of them follow nothing but conjecture. Certainly, conjecture can be of no avail against the truth. Surely, Allah is All-Aware of what they do" (10:35-36).

From the above—and from numerous other arguments and proofs scattered throughout the Quran—one should conclude that there is nothing worthy of worship except Allah. Consequently, if there is nothing worthy of worship except Allah, it is rational for the individual to insist upon himself that he worships no one other than Allah. This is actually the key message of all of Islam and the message that all of the prophets preached. This is what is captured in the first part of the Islamic testimony of faith, "I bear witness that there is none worthy of worship except Allah."

At this point, though, it is important to clarify the meaning of this term "worship" from an Islamic perspective. The word translated as "worship" here is the Quranic and Arabic term *ibaadah*. This term has very different connotations from the English word "worship."

The *Oxford English Dictionary* defines worship as, "To honour or revere as a supernatural being or power, or as a holy thing; to regard or approach with veneration; to adore with appropriate acts, rites, or ceremonies."[1] The lexical root of the word in English means "to honor" and, thus, it can be further defined in English as, "the performance of devotional acts in honor of a deity."[2] But, as Bilal Philips notes,

> However, in the language of the final revelation, Arabic, worship is called *'ibaadah* which is derived from the noun *'abd* meaning "a slave." A slave is one who is expected to do whatever his master wills. Consequently, worship according to the final revelation means "obedient submission to the will of God." This was the essence of the message of all the prophets sent by God to humankind. For example, this understanding of worship was emphatically expressed by Prophet Jesus in the Gospel according to Matthew, 7:21, "None of those who call me 'Lord' will enter the kingdom of God, but only the one who does the will of my Father in heaven."[3]

Thus, this aspect of monotheism—the belief in Allah as the only object of worship—goes well beyond the concept of worship as understood by many in the West, in particular. This aspect of monotheism has been defined by al-Saadi in the following terms,

> Is to know and recognize with knowledge and certainty that Allah is the only God and the only one truly deserving of worship. [It is also to verify

---

[1] *Oxford English Dictionary* (Oxford University Press, CD Rom Version 3.0, 2002).

[2] Bilal Philips, *The Purpose of Creation* (Sharjah, UAE: Dar al Fatah, 1995), p. 40.

[3] Bilal Philips, *The Purpose*, pp. 41-42.

that] the attributes of Godhood and its meaning are not found in any of [Allah's] creatures. No one is then deserving of worship except Allah. If the person recognizes that and recognizes it correctly, he will reserve all of his external and internal acts of servitude and worship for Allah alone. He will fulfill the external acts of Islam, such as prayer, fasting,… striving [for His sake], ordering good and eradicating evil, being dutiful to parents, keeping the ties of kinship, fulfilling the rights of Allah and the rights of His creatures… He will not have any goal in life other than pleasing His Lord and attaining His rewards. In his affairs, he will be following the Messenger of Allah (peace be upon him). His beliefs will be whatever is proven in the Quran and sunnah. His deeds and actions will be what Allah and His Messenger legislated. His character and manners will be in imitation of His prophet, in his guidance, behavior and all of his affairs.[1]

This aspect of Islamic monotheism comprises both the feelings in the heart as well as the deeds of the physical body. The feelings in the heart include putting all of one's trust and reliance in Him alone, having utmost fear of Him alone, having utmost hope in Him alone, having contentment with Him as God and Creator and so forth.

In fact, there are two aspects in particular that must be combined in the worship of Allah. Al-Saadi further stated,

The spirit and actuality of worship is by the realization of love and submission to Allah. Complete love and full submission to Allah is the reality of worship. If the act of worship is missing both or one of those components, it is not truly an

---

[1] Abdul Rahman Al-Saadi, *Al-Fatawa al-Saadiyah* (Riyadh: Manshooraat al-Muassasat al-Saeediyah, n.d), pp. 10-11.

act of worship. For the reality of worship is found in submission and yielding to Allah. And that will only occur if there is complete and full love [for Allah] which dominates all other expressions of love.[1]

From the above, it is clear that the belief in Allah as the only object of worship actually has a number of corresponding corollaries by which one must abide. In particular, there are a number of aspects of life that must be solely "dedicated to" Allah. Without an understanding of this fact, one has failed to grasp the reality of the statement, "There is none worthy of worship except Allah." A brief explanation of these aspects should make this concept clearer.

First, all ritual acts of worship must be directed solely to Allah alone. Prayers, fasting, pilgrimage, alms and so forth must be done solely with the intent of pleasing Allah and as acts of worship towards Him alone. Thus, for example, if anyone prays to anyone other than Allah, he is actually violating the principles of worshipping no one other than Allah. In fact, the Prophet (peace and blessings of Allah be upon him) stated, "Prayers are the [essence of] worship."[2]

Second, all ultimate authority in life rests with Allah. In other words, one must submit oneself only to the commands and revelation coming from Allah. He is the Creator and He has the right to lay down legislation and laws for the guidance of humankind. "The dominion [of rule and judgment] is for none but Allah. He has commanded that you worship none but Him, that is the [true] straight religion" (*Yusuf* 40). Intentionally ignoring or arrogantly superseding the laws from God means that one is not truly submitting to God and, thus, one is not taking Him as the only object of worship and submission. In fact, Allah makes it clear that some of the previous communities erred when it came to this very issue. Allah says, "They

---

[1] Quoted in Muhammad al-Hammad, *Tauheed al-Uloohiyah* (Dar ibn Khuzaima, 1414 A.H.), p. 26.

[2] Recorded by Abu Dawud, al-Nasai, al-Tirmidhi and others.

(Jews and Christians) took their rabbis and their monks to be their lords besides Allah [by obeying them in things which they made lawful or unlawful according to their own desires without being ordered by Allah], and (they also took as their Lord) Messiah, son of Mary, while they were commanded to worship none but One God. None has the right to be worshipped but He. Praise and glory be to Him, (far above is He) from having the partners they associate (with Him)" (9:31).

Third, one's loves, loyalties, likes and dislikes must be in accord with what Allah has revealed. This aspect flows from the heart when the heart is truly filled with the belief in, love of and adoration for Allah alone. It is a fairly simple concept but it has far-reaching implications. The completeness of faith requires that Allah is the most beloved thing in one's heart—He is *the* beloved of soul. When this fact permeates the human, he begins to love what his beloved loves and dislike what his beloved dislikes. Although this is commonplace with respect to the relations between humans, this phenomenon is more intense and comprehensive when found in the relationship between a human and his Lord. Thus, if Allah is found to love something, the devoted worshipper and servant also loves that thing. Conversely, if Allah is found to detest something—although He has created it and put it in this world as a test for humans and made it available to them—the devoted worshipper and servant will also detest that thing. Of course, the key to all of this is in the revelation from God Himself. If God states that He loves purity, sincerity, goodness and charity, for example, then these are beloved to the Muslim. If God demonstrates or states a dislike for idol worship, adultery, homosexuality, drinking alcohol and so on, then the devoted believer immediately develops and has a dislike for all of these displeasing acts. All of this is part of his believing in Allah as the only object of worship and adoration.

Although accepting Allah as the only object of worship is the essential aspect of true monotheism, it is a concept that is not always understood in its totality nor applied in its proper manner. This is a real loss for humans because it is this aspect of monotheism that is *the key* to a "real life", a life that is sound and proper. Ibn Taimiya wrote,

> You must know that a human's need for Allah— that he worship Him and not associate any partner with Him— is a need concerning which there is no comparison that one can make an analogy to. In some matters, it resembles the need of the body for food and drink. However, there are many differences between the two.
>
> The reality of a human being is in his heart and soul. These cannot be prosperous except through [their relation] with Allah, concerning whom there is no other god. There is[, for example,] no tranquility in this world except in His remembrance. Verily, man is heading toward his Lord and he shall meet Him. He must definitely meet Him. There is no true goodness for him except in meeting Him.[1] If the human experiences any pleasure or happiness other than in Allah, that joy and happiness will not endure. It will move from one nature to another or from one person to another. The person will enjoy it at one time or only some of the time. In fact, sometimes the thing he enjoys and gets pleasure from does not bring him pleasure or enjoyment. Sometimes it even hurts him when it comes to him, and he is even more harmed by that. But his God is definitely always with him under every circumstance and at all times. Wherever he is, He is with him [by His knowledge and aid]…
>
> If someone worships anything other than Allah— even if he loves it and attains some love in this

---

[1] This is because the soul, by its ingrained nature, yearns for its meeting with its Creator.

world and some form of pleasure from that— [that false worship] will destroy the person in a way greater than the harmful displeasure that comes to a person who took poison...[1]

Again, it cannot be emphasized enough that the belief in only one Creator and Sustainer of the cosmos is not all there is to a proper belief in God. Throughout history, it has been the case that some people stopped at this clear premise and deemed that such was all there was to the belief in God. Nothing could be further from the reality. That belief is definitely necessary but it is not sufficient. That belief must be followed up with the proper relations, emotions of the heart and acts with respect to Allah. It is by these acts that one truly takes the Creator as his only "God," meaning his only object of extreme love, adoration and submission. In so doing, he denies that anyone other than Allah deserves to be worshipped in any way. Then, and only then, he will be fulfilling what it truly means to believe in God.

In sum, based on the preceding facts: (1) the human should desire to worship Allah due to His greatness and perfection and the fact that He is the only Creator and Sustainer; (2) Allah alone has these attributes just described and hence He alone deserves to be worshipped; and (3) the human should refrain from worshipping anything other than Allah in any shape or form.

There is one final but important point that needs to be added at the end of these two sections: Since the signs for the true belief in God are so strong (in human nature, in the physical surroundings, in the messages taught by the prophets throughout the ages) it is completely unacceptable rationally and religiously to worship anyone other than God. Hence, such associating of partners with God[2] or

---

[1] Ahmad Ibn Taimiya, *Majmoo Fatawaa Shaikh al-Islaam ibn Taimiya* (Collected by Abdul Rahmaan Qaasim and his son Muhammad. No publication information given), vol. 1, pp. 24-29.

[2] Polytheism means coupling the worship of God with the worship of idols, trees, animals, graves, heavenly bodies, natural powers, and so on. It also means the acceptance of

refusal to worship God is a sin whose enormity and arrogance is so great that if one dies in such a state, Allah will not forgive that sin. Allah has clearly stated, "Verily, Allah forgives not that partners should be set up with him in worship, but He forgives except that (anything else) to whom He pleases, and whoever sets up partners with Allah in worship, he has indeed invented a tremendous sin" (4:48, see also 4:116).

Belief in Allah's Names and Attributes

To truly be devoted to Allah and to love Allah above all else imaginable one needs to have knowledge about Allah that goes beyond the basic aspects of Him being the sole Creator and Sustainer. Indeed, a believer would yearn to know more and more about Allah.[1] Of course, Allah is beyond the realm of human experience and therefore one cannot accurately know details about God unless He reveals them. Via His revelation and by His grace and mercy, Allah has revealed a great deal of information about Himself, such that any truth seeker can know and worship his Lord based on accurate knowledge.

In fact, the Prophet (peace and blessings of Allah be upon him) stated, "Allah has ninety-nine names, one hundred less one." Thus, one finds Allah's names and attributes mentioned throughout the Quran. For example, Allah says, "He is Allah other than Whom there is none who has the right to be worshipped, the King, the Holy, the One Free from all defects, the Giver of security, the Watcher over His creatures, the All-Mighty, the Compeller, the Supreme. Glory be to Allah! (High is He) above all that they associate as partners with Him.   He is Allah, the Creator, the Inventor of all things, the Bestower of forms. To Him belong the Best Names. All that is in the heavens and the earth glorify Him. And He is the All-Mighty, the

---

individuals or prophets as gods, or the pretence that Almighty God has sons and daughters. See Tabbarah, p. 47.

[1] It is perhaps this yearning that has led to personalized gods, gods that humans can touch, "humanized" gods, human "sons" of god and other anthropomorphic beliefs. However, these false beliefs bring nothing but misery in the end as they result in associating partners with Allah, a grievous sin that is unforgivable if one dies while committing it.

All-Wise" (59:23-24). In another verse, mentioned by the Prophet himself as the greatest verse of the Quran, Allah is further described in marvelous detail: "Allah! None has the right to be worshipped but He, the Ever Living, the One Who sustains and protects all that exists. Neither slumber, nor sleep overtake Him. To Him belongs whatever is in the heavens and whatever is on earth. Who is he that can intercede with Him except with His Permission? He knows what happens to them (His creatures) in this world, and what will happen to them in the Hereafter. And they will never compass anything of His Knowledge except that which He wills. His Footstool extends over the heavens and the earth, and He feels no fatigue in guarding and preserving them. And He is the Most High, the Most Great" (2:255).

From the Quran and statements of the Prophet (peace and blessings of Allah be upon him) one can learn the following about Allah: Allah is the Most Compassionate, Ever Merciful[1], Ever Forgiving, Ever accepting of repentance, Ever Patient, Pardoning and Loving.[2] He is the Generous, the Magnanimous, the Bestower and the

---

[1] Muslims remain constantly aware of Allah and of these two of His names in particular. Before beginning virtually any act, a Muslim states, "In the name of Allah, the Most Compassionate, the Ever Merciful."

[2] On this point it should be noted that there are some who try to attack Islam by claiming that Islam does not believe in a personalized or loving God. Christians, for example, quote their Bible, I John 4:8, "He that loveth not knoweth not God; for God is love" (*King James Version*). James Coffman's *New Testament Commentary* states, "No one in the whole world ever knew that God is love until it was revealed from heaven and written in the New Testament. 'It is here, and nowhere else; it is not found in all the literature of mankind.'" (Taken from *The Bible Collection CD*.) This passage, of course, is problematic. Even when this author was a Christian, he could not find a satisfactory answer as to what the expression, "God is love," truly means. Love is simply an abstract concept. How could God be love? For example, if two people fall out of love, does that mean that God is in any way diminished? If two people have a forbidden love, is that still God or His presence? This author has never been offered reasonable answers to these and similar questions. On the other hand, to say that God is "loving" or that He is the source of positive love makes perfect sense. This means that this is one of His attributes. The Quran states that Allah is *al-Wadood* (85:14), meaning, "The loving, affectionate, giver of love." Furthermore, the Quran repeatedly emphasizes that Allah is *al-Rahmaan* and *al-Raheem* (the Most

Clement. He responds to those who call upon Him and He is the Rescuer. He is the Glorious, the Great, the deserver of all Praise, Lord of all creation, Master of the Day of Judgment and the Judge of the Final reckoning. He is the All-Hearing, the All-Seeing, the All-Knowing and the All-Wise. He is the Ever Strong, Ever Capable, Almighty. He is the Self-Sufficient, free of any need and provider of all sustenance. He is the Exalted and the Most High. He is the Watcher over all affairs and the Protector. He is administering the affairs of His creation, commanding, forbidding, being pleased, being angered, rewarding, punishing, giving, withholding, honoring, debasing. He does whatever He wills. He is attributed with every attribute of perfection and free of even the tiniest amount of imperfection or shortcoming. Greatly exalted and perfect is He above all that they associate with Him. Not even an atom moves save by His will and permission.

This wonderful information about Allah Himself is a great blessing for humankind. There is no need for humans to try to ponder over the nature of God while, as stated above, God is above their comprehension. Instead of deriving fanciful theories about God, God Himself has revealed sufficient information about Himself that humankind need not stray or be confused. Furthermore, He has provided the information in such a way that all can understand it, even though one can imagine that it is simply the tip of the iceberg of the depths of the greatness of the Lord and Creator.

On this point, though, there is something very clear in the Quran: There is absolutely no hint of any form of anthropomorphism in the Islamic beliefs about God. This is a point concerning which many earlier peoples have strayed. The famous humorous but true statement made by many in the West, "God created man in His own image and man was quick to return the favor," has no place within Islamic beliefs. The Creator and the created are separate and distinct. The attributes of Allah are perfect attributes that are becoming of His

---

Compassionate, the Ever Merciful), which are concepts that actually go above and beyond the simple concept of love.

holiness and greatness. Even when there is some "common concept" between an attribute of Allah and an attribute of humans, there is actually no similarity in the quality of the two. Thus, Allah Himself says in the Quran, "There is nothing like unto Him, and He is the All-Hearer, the All-Seeing" (42:11). Here, there is a complete denial of anthropomorphism while at the same time affirming that Allah hears and sees. Muslims always realize Allah's perfection while never belittling Him by describing Him in unbecoming manners. God does not have human-like attributes nor do humans have Divine attributes. Any violation of this latter principle is clear disbelief and associating of partners with Allah.[1]

People before the coming of the Prophet (peace be upon him) accepted the idea of Allah being the only Creator of the Universe. However, they associated partners with Allah in different forms of worship. Therefore, Islam came to purify this concept of Allah being the Lord and gave it its proper understanding. Thus, the beginning point is to have knowledge and correct understanding of Allah's names and attributes. If one has knowledge of and a correct understanding of Allah's names and attributes, then he would never turn to anyone else or direct any form of worship to anyone other than Allah.

Furthermore, the knowledge and understanding of these names and attributes should play a profound role in the development and purification of the soul. In reality, the knowledge of each of

---

[1] Unfortunately, the books of the Jews and Christians have become sullied by numerous anthropomorphic passages. For example, In Genesis 32:24-28, there is the story and literal description of Jacob wrestling with and defeating God. In verse 28, it says, "You [Jacob] have wrestled with God and with men, and you have won." In other words, the creator of the universe whom mankind is expected to worship and submit to was defeated by a mere mortal in a wrestling match. In numerous places the picture of God in the Old Testament is not that of a great and perfect being. In fact, the Old Testament even pictures God as one who intended to do evil but then repented. Exodus 32:14 states, "And the Lord repented of the evil which he thought to do unto his people" (*King James Version*). The Christian conception of God and God having a son is, of course, completely blasphemous from an Islamic perspective. For more details on this point, see the author's *Purification of the Soul: Concept, Process and Means*, pp. 20-29.

Allah's names should lead a person to greater love of Allah as well as greater fear of Him, accompanied by attempting to get closer to Him due to His wonderful attributes of perfection and greatness.

Additionally, a detailed knowledge about God is going to have a greater effect on the individual than a general, vague knowledge about God. Many of the great scholars of Islam emphasized this point. For example, Ibn Taimiyyah noted, "Whoever knows the names of Allah and their meanings, while believing in them, will have a more complete faith than the one who does not know them but just believes in them in general."[1] Ibn Saadi also stated, "Whenever a person's knowledge of Allah's beautiful names and attributes increases, his faith also increases and his certainty is further strengthened."[2]

There is an important and vital relationship between this concept of Allah's names and attributes and the previous two concepts (the belief that God is the Sole Creator and Sustainer of all Creation and the belief that Allah must be the only object of worship). One could argue that deviations with respect to monotheism are rooted in a failure to understand and appreciate the names and attributes of Allah as well as their uniqueness. If one honestly recognized and understood the names and attributes of Allah, one would never have any desire to worship or submit to anything other than Allah himself.

From the history of humankind[3], it can be argued that it is innate in humans that they would want to worship. They want to have a god that they can worship and adore. They know that there must be something special and great about that thing which they humble themselves to. However, so many of them put their hopes, trust, dreams and aspirations in things that are simply not deserving of such—whether it be forces of nature, inanimate objects, other

---

[1] Ahmad ibn Taimiyyah, *Majmoo Fatawaa Shaikh al-Islaam ibn Taimiya*, vol. 7, p. 234.

[2] Quoted in Fauz bint Abdul Lateef al-Kurdi, *Tahqeeq al-Uboodiyyah bi-Marifah al-Asmaa wa al-Sifaat* (Riyadh: Daar Taibah, 1421 A.H.), p. 164.

[3] Not to speak of the proofs from the Quran and Sunnah.

humans, materialism, nations, race, whatever. They force themselves to believe that these false objects of worship can bring about what they hope for and what they are dreaming of. In other words, they begin to give their false objects of worship the attributes of God. Instead of turning to God and knowing God by His attributes—and then realizing that He is the One they are truly looking for—they turn to other objects of worship, love and adoration. Due to this, they stray very far from the straight path and from their true God.

In numerous places, Allah speaks about such gross errors. Upon closer inspection, it can be noted that the source of their errors is incorrect belief about the attributes of those that they turn to while ignoring the attributes that reside with Allah. For example, Allah says, "Say [O Muhammad to mankind], 'How do you worship besides Allah something which has no power either to harm or to benefit you? But it is Allah Who is the All-Hearer, All-Knower'" (5:76). Allah also says, "And who is more astray than one who calls (invokes) besides Allah, such as will not answer him till the Day of Resurrection, and who are (even) unaware of their calls (invocations) to them?   And when mankind are gathered (on the Day of Resurrection), they (false deities) will become enemies for them and will deny their worshipping" (46:5-6). Allah also says, "And they worship others besides Allah, such as do not and cannot own any provision for them from the heavens or the earth" (16:73). Again, "Is then He, Who creates as one who creates not? Will you not then receive admonition?" (16:17). And, as a final example, "O mankind! A similitude has been coined, so listen to it (carefully): Verily! Those on whom you call besides Allah, cannot create (even) a fly, even though they combine together for the purpose. And if the fly snatched away a thing from them, they would have no power to release it from the fly. So weak are (both) the seeker and the sought. They have not estimated Allah His Rightful Estimate; Verily, Allah is All-Strong, All-Mighty" (22:73-74)

In reality, it is Allah who hears, Allah who responds, Allah who gives, Allah who is in control, Allah who is the just and the judge, Allah who creates, sustains, gives, recreates and so forth. In sum, if one truly knows the names and attributes of Allah, one would never turn to worship anyone or anything but Him. None of those false objects of worship are deserving of worship. By worshipping them and seeking them, humans are doing nothing but debasing themselves. Worse of all, they are ignoring Allah, equating partners with Him, earning His wrath and preparing for themselves an evil end.

Summary

The proper belief in Allah is the essence and cornerstone of the Islamic faith. It is the key—the key to life, the key to proper living, the key to understanding reality, the key to happiness and peace. When the person truly knows Allah, he will recognize that it does not make any sense to worship anything other than Him. He will realize that this is what his soul has been created for and this is what it has been seeking. Once he realizes the beauty of worshipping Allah alone, he will never desire or wish to worship anyone other than Him. His soul will be a rest and his heart will be tranquil.

The Cosmos
The Creation of the Cosmos and How it Points to Allah's Existence

The cosmos or integrated and whole universe is made up of various parts. There are the galaxies and solar systems that are above and beyond earth. On earth, there are inanimate objects, such as the mountains, oceans and land. There is also the animal kingdom with all its great varieties. There are aspects of creation that humans are still discovering and coming across today. All of these are actually part and parcel of the creative work of God.

In the Quran, it is clear that it was Allah Who created the heavens and the earth. For example, Allah says, "He has created the heavens and the earth with truth. High be He Exalted above all they associate as partners with Him" (16:3). "He has created the heavens and the earth with truth. He makes the night to go in the day and makes the day to go in the night. And He has subjected the sun and the moon. Each running (on a fixed course) for an appointed term. Verily, He is the All-Mighty, the Oft-Forgiving" (39:5). In sum, Allah says, "Allah is the Creator of all things, and He is the Disposer of affairs over all things" (39:62).

Allah's power to create is beyond comprehension. It is simply a matter of Him giving the command and the object is created. Allah says, "[Allah] the Originator of the heavens and the earth. When He decrees a matter, He only says to it, 'Be!'—and behold it is" (2:117; also see 36:82 and 40:68). He is the One who created, shaped, determined portions and guided the different parts of the creation. Allah says, "Glorify the Name of your Lord, the Most High, Who has created (everything), and then proportioned it; And Who has measured; then guided" (87:1-3).

Allah has also stated that He created the heavens and the earth in six stages. "Allah it is He Who has created the heavens and the earth, and all that is between them in six Days.[1] Then He rose over

---

[1] The Arabic word *ayaam* translated above as "Days" does not necessarily refer to twenty-four hour periods. Instead, they are six periods of time. Elsewhere, for example, Allah says,

the Throne [in a manner that suits His Majesty]. You [humankind] have none, besides Him, as a protector or an intercessor. Will you not then remember (or be admonished)?" (32:4; also see 7:54; 10:3; 11:7; 25:59).

In the section entitled, "The Belief that God is the Sole Creator and Sustainer of all Creation," there was a lengthy discussion of how the make-up of this creation clearly points to the fact that there is only one Creator and Sustainer. There is no need to repeat that discussion here. However, some other very important points can be derived from pondering over this creation.

In numerous verses of the Quran, Allah points to different aspects of the creation and describes them as signs for those people who reflect.[1] For example, Allah says, "And it is He Who spread out the earth, and placed therein firm mountains and rivers and of every kind of fruits He made two in pairs. He brings the night as a cover over the day. Verily, in these things, there are signs for people who reflect" (13:3). "He it is Who sends down water (rain) from the sky; from it you drink and from it (grows) the vegetation on which you send your cattle to pasture; With it He causes to grow for you the crops, the olives, the date-palms, the grapes, and every kind of fruit. Verily! In this is indeed an evident proof and a manifest sign for people who give thought. And He has subjected to you the night and the day, the sun and the moon; and the stars are subjected by His Command. Surely, in this are proofs for people who understand. And whatsoever He has created for you on this earth of varying colors. Verily! In this is a sign for people who remember" (16:10-13). As a

---

"And verily, a day with your Lord is as a thousand years of what you reckon" (22:47). See also 32:5. In yet another verse, Allah says, "The angels and the Spirit [Gabriel] ascend to Him in a Day the measure whereof is fifty thousand years" (70:4). More on the creation will be given in the section on the scientific miracles in the Quran and Sunnah.

[1] Note that this is a clear sign that the religion of truth does not fear science in any way. In the West, faith has often been pitted against science. However, that false competition is due to the nature of the religion that most people follow in the West. It has nothing to do necessarily with religion as a whole and certainly not with the true religion that comes from the same Creator who created the heavens and the earth.

final example, Allah also says, "Verily! In the creation of the heavens and the earth, and in the alternation of night and day, and the ships which sail through the sea with that which is of use to mankind, and the water (rain) which Allah sends down from the sky and makes the earth alive therewith after its death, and the moving (living) creatures of all kinds that He has scattered therein, and in the veering of winds and clouds which are held between the sky and the earth, are indeed signs for people of understanding" (2:164).

In the hustle and bustle of today's world, many find little time to reflect upon this creation, their presence in this creation and any purpose behind it all. However, it is important that people take the time to reflect and think. When they do so, they will find signs and lessons that will bring them straight back to God—a most important step in their lives. The signs are actually all around them, if they would only reflect upon them. Thus, God says, "We will show them Our Signs in the universe, and in their own selves, until it becomes manifest to them that this (the Quran) is the truth. Is it not sufficient in regard to your Lord that He is a Witness over all things?" (41:53).

Reflecting upon the intricacy and order of this creation makes one realize that there must be some purpose behind this creation. It is unimaginable that any being would make something with such precision and perfection and yet there would be no rhyme or reason to the whole creation.[1] This is a point that Allah makes in numerous places in the Quran. For example, Allah says, "We created not the heavens and the earth and all that is between them for a (mere) play" (21:16). Allah also says, "Verily! In the creation of the heavens and the earth, and in the alternation of night and day, there are indeed signs for men of understanding. Those who remember Allah (always, and in prayers) standing, sitting, and lying down on their sides, and think deeply about the creation of the heavens and the earth, (saying): 'Our Lord! You have not created (all) this without purpose, glory to

---

[1] Of course, this is what materialists claim. They claim that everything is a result of mere chance and interaction of molecules. Hence, there could be no purpose behind any of this marvelous creation. Their views shall be discussed shortly.

You! (Exalted be You above all that they associate with You as partners). Give us salvation from the torment of the Fire'" (3:190-191). Allah also says, "Do they not think deeply (in their own selves) about themselves? Allah has created not the heavens and the earth, and all that is between them, except with truth and for an appointed term. And indeed many of mankind deny the Meeting with their Lord" (30:8). Again, Allah says, "Did you think that We had created you in play (without any purpose), and that you would not be brought back to Us?" (23:115).

The Quranic argument is that it is not logically possible to come to any other conclusion. Indeed, if a person believes in God as the Creator, by definition it is unbecoming of such a noble and great to create all of this order and beauty and yet have no purpose behind that creation. A person who believes in a creator yet believes that this creator had no purpose or thought behind his creation is describing a creator that is childlike and unintelligent. It is hard to believe that a creator like that could possibly come up with a creation like the one that everyone witnesses today. No, indeed, the creation points to certain attributes of the Creator and it points to there being an important and great purpose behind this entire creation. The whole nature of the existence points to the Creator being one of very special character who would not create anything of this nature simply in sport or jest. That Creator could only be Allah with His perfect and sublime attributes—that is, this creation needs Allah and it could not be just and proper except under the control of Allah, exactly as Allah is. Thus, Allah says in the Quran, "Had there been therein (in the heavens and the earth) gods besides Allah, then verily they both[1] would have been ruined. Glorified be Allah, the Lord of the Throne, (High is He) above what they attribute to Him" (21:22).

A second very important conclusion that one can derive by simply pondering over this creation is that the one who created this from nothing can easily recreate it. If He has the ability to recreate things even after their demise, this also means that He has the ability

---

[1] Meaning both the heavens and the earth.

to resurrect them and bring them all in front of Him. This thought, obviously, has very ominous repercussions for humans and their behavior in this world. Thus, Allah points out this fact and reminds humans of its meaning throughout the Quran.

For example, Allah says, "See they not that Allah, Who created the heavens and the earth, is Able to create the like of them. And He has decreed for them an appointed term, whereof there is no doubt. But the wrong-doers refuse [the truth and accept nothing] but disbelief" (17:99). Another set of verses state, "And he [the human] puts forth for Us a parable, and forgets his own creation. He says, 'Who will give life to these bones when they have rotted away and became dust?' Say (to them O Muhammad), 'He will give life to them Who created them for the first time! And He is the All-Knower of every creation! He, Who produces for you fire out of the green tree, when behold, You kindle therewith. Is not He, Who created the heavens and the earth Able to create the like of them? Yes, indeed! He is the All-Knowing Supreme Creator. Verily, His Command, when He intends a thing, is only that He says to it, 'Be!' and it is! So Glorified is He and Exalted above all that they associate with Him, and in Whose Hands is the dominion of all things, and to Him you shall be returned" (36:78-83).

In another passage, Allah states, "Look then at the effects (results) of Allah's Mercy, how He revives the earth after its death. Verily! That (Allah) Who revived the earth after its death shall indeed raise the dead (on the Day of Resurrection), and He is Able to do all things" (30:50). Yet again Allah says, "And among His proofs is the creation of the heavens and the earth, and whatever moving (living) creatures He has dispersed in them both. And He is All-Potent over their assembling [i.e. resurrecting them on the Day of Resurrection after their death, and dispersion of their bodies] whenever He will" (42:29) Another verse reads, "And He it is Who originates the creation, then will repeat it (after it has been perished), and this is easier for Him. His is the highest description in the heavens and in the earth. And He is the All-Mighty, the All-Wise"

(30:27). And, as a final example, Allah says, "Do they not understand that Allah, Who created the heavens and the earth, and was not wearied by their creation, is Able to give life to the dead? Yes, He surely is Able to do all things" (46:33).

Thus, this creation is a clear sign—when added to the fact that there must be a purpose behind this creation—of the Resurrection. The concept of the Resurrection is not something that violates nature but it is completely consistent with nature. Allah points this out in the following moving passage that not only points out the arrogance of those who refuse to see the truth but that also points out the result of their own actions:

> O mankind! If you are in doubt about the Resurrection, then verily We have created you (i.e. Adam) from dust, then from mixed drops of male and female sexual discharge, then from a clot (a piece of thick coagulated blood) then from a little lump of flesh, some formed and some unformed (miscarriage), that We may make (it) clear to you (i.e. to show you Our Power and Ability to do what We will). And We cause whom We will to remain in the wombs for an appointed term, then We bring you out as infants, then (give you growth) that you may reach your age of full strength. And among you there is he who dies (young), and among you there is he who is brought back to the miserable old age, so that he knows nothing after having known. And you see the earth barren, but when We send down water (rain) on it, it is stirred (to life), it swells and puts forth every lovely kind (of growth). That is because Allah, He is the Truth, and it is He Who gives life to the dead, and it is He Who is Able to do all things. And surely, the Hour is coming, there is no doubt about it, and certainly, Allah will resurrect those who are in the graves. And among

men is he who disputes about Allah, without
knowledge or guidance, or a Book giving light
(from Allah), Bending his neck in pride (far astray
from the Path of Allah), and leading (others) too
(far) astray from the Path of Allah. For him there is
disgrace in this worldly life, and on the Day of
Resurrection We shall make him taste the torment
of burning (Fire). That is because of what your
hands have sent forth, and verily, Allah is not
unjust to (His) slaves (22:5-10).

The one who negates the resurrection is expecting that Allah
will treat the wrongdoers like the pious people. This is an
unbecoming expectation of Allah. Allah makes it clear that such will
never be the case, highlighting that such thoughts can only come
from those who disbelieve in God. Allah says, "And We created not
the heaven and the earth and all that is between them without
purpose! That is the consideration of those who disbelieve! Then woe
to those who disbelieve from the Fire! Shall We treat those who
believe and do righteous good deeds, as the evildoers on earth? Or
shall We treat the pious as the wicked?" (38:27-28).

After so many signs in the creation and so many reminders
and lessons in the revelation one must ask: What will be the human's
excuse if he does not respond in the proper manner to the evidence all
around him? Is it not expected that he will not have a valid excuse?
Then won't it be just for Allah to treat him as someone who
obstinately and arrogantly rejected so many signs that he does not
even deserve leniency in the end?

The Wisdom Behind the Creation of the Cosmos

Following from the above and earlier discussions, one can
discern some of the wisdom behind the creation of the cosmos. These
can be delineated in the following points:

(1) The existence of the creation and the nature of this
creation points to the existence of the Creator, as discussed in the
previous chapter.

(2) The magnitude, perfection and detail of this universe point to a purpose behind this creation. It would be unbecoming the Wise Creator to create something of this nature with no purpose or reason behind it.

(3) The initial creation also indicates Allah's ability to recreate. The One who created from nothing can easily recreate what He has already created. This is a warning and sign of the coming of the Resurrection.

The above three points were all discussed in either the previous chapter or earlier in this chapter. There are yet other important points behind the creation of this cosmos.

The creation of the cosmos brings forth or manifests many of the attributes of Allah. This in itself is a beautiful, wondrous and desirable thing. For example, Allah always had the ability to create but until He created, this attribute was not manifested in any concrete manner. Of course, the manner in which He creates points to many of His other sublime attributes. They demonstrate His complete ability, His power, His wisdom and knowledge (as reflected in the balance in the creation) and His greatness. Without the creation of the cosmos, these wonderful attributes would have existed but they would not have been exhibited or appreciated. This demonstrates that it was great and wonderful of Allah to create this cosmos.

In reality, everything of this creation submits to the will and command of Allah, highlighting His nature and attributes of greatness and dominion. The creation knows the reality of Allah and does not refuse to bow and submit to Him alone—except for some humans[1], as shall be explained shortly. Allah says, "And to Allah prostate all that is in the heavens and all that is in the earth, of the live moving creatures and the angels, and they are not proud [they worship their Lord (Allah) with humility]" (16:49).

There is yet another great purpose behind the creation of the cosmos. The different aspects of this creation are meant to be at the

---

[1] As well as some jinn. Jinn are another creation that Allah has created with limited free-will. In general, jinn, like angels, are not seen by humans.

service of one of the creatures: humankind. This is a specific blessing from Allah to this creature. Allah says in the Quran, "See you not (O men) that Allah has subjected for you whatsoever is in the heavens and whatsoever is in the earth, and has completed and perfected His Graces upon you, (both) apparent and hidden? Yet of mankind is he who disputes about Allah without knowledge or guidance or a Book giving light!" (31:20). He also said, "And has subjected to you all that is in the heavens and all that is in the earth; it is all as a favor and kindness from Him. Verily, in it are signs for a people who think deeply" (45:13).[1]

This is a great blessing and a great responsibility. These verses in no way imply that man is free to deal with these resources in any way that he wills. The Prophet (peace and blessings of Allah be upon him) said, "The world is sweet and green (alluring) and Allah is going to put you in charge of it to see how you will behave. So beware of the worldly things..." One can see that this great bounty comes with great responsibility. In other words, there is some way or purpose for which the creation is to be put to use. Thus, the question is: For what reason or purpose did Allah put all of these resources at the disposal of humankind? Before giving an answer to this question, a discussion of the relationship between humans and the rest of the creation is proper.

Humans and the Creation[2]

The previous discussion demonstrates that there is something distinct and special about this creation known as humans. However, the original, physical creation of the first human was not greatly different from the creation of the other creatures of this world. The physical make-up of the first human, Adam, was from clay and water, two of the already created substances of this cosmos. This fact is noted in numerous places in the Quran. For example, Allah says, "And it is He Who has created man from water, and has appointed

---

[1] Also see 14:32-33; 16:12; and 22:65.

[2] Some of the material in this section is borrowed from the author's *Purification of the Soul*, pp. 23-25 and 107-113.

for him kindred by blood, and kindred by marriage. And your Lord is Ever All- Powerful to do what He will" (25:54). Allah also says, "And indeed, We created man from sounding clay of altered black smooth mud" (15:26).

It is in the next stage of the creation of the first human, Adam, in which the real distinction occurred. At this point, humans are made a very separate and unique creature, combining a physical aspect and a special spiritual aspect that God bestowed on them. In fact, this is what makes them very different from the other living creatures on this same planet. This stage is described in the verse, "Then He fashioned him in due proportion, and breathed into him the soul, and He gave you hearing (ears), sight (eyes) and hearts. Little is the thanks you give" (32:9).

Even before Allah created this creation, He informed the angels that this creation was to have a special purpose on this earth, succeeding the creations before him. Allah says, "Behold, your Lord said to the angels, 'I will create upon the earth a successive authority'" (2:30). After Allah breathed into this creation with a spirit from Him and after He had bestowed knowledge upon him, the angels, Allah's noble creation, were ordered to prostrate to this new creation. Allah says, for example, "So, when I have fashioned him completely and breathed into him (Adam) the soul which I created for him, then fall (you) down prostrating yourselves unto him" (15.29).

Allah tells humankind about another difference between humans and the remainder of creation. Allah states that humans on their own opted to accept the responsibility of the trust of free will and moral responsibility. Other creations were offered this heavy responsibility but they all refused. It was only humans who took this job on. Allah describes this occurrence in the following verse. Allah says, "Truly, We did offer the trust [or moral responsibility and all the duties which Allah has ordained] to the heavens and the earth, and the mountains, but they declined to bear it and were afraid of it. But man bore it. Verily, he was unjust (to himself) and ignorant (of its results)" (33:72). This is why it can be seen that everything in the cosmos submits to and bows down to Allah, willingly and submissively, except for a section of humankind and jinn. These have to submit to Allah's cosmic laws whether they wish to or not but they have been giving a realm of freedom of will, wherein they may decide not to submit to Allah's moral laws. Thus, Allah says, "See you not that to Allah prostrates whoever is in the heavens and whoever is on the earth, and the sun, and the moon, and the stars, and the mountains, and the trees, and moving living creature, and many of mankind? But there are many (men) on whom the punishment is justified. And whomsoever Allah disgraces, none can honor him. Verily! Allah does what He wills" (22:18).

Although mankind took on a heavy responsibility, Allah then helped mankind in many ways to fulfill this trust—Allah is ever Merciful and Compassionate. (Allah will also reward mankind in a special fashion when they fulfill this trust—Allah is ever generous and appreciative of good efforts.) That is, along with this great responsibility that humankind took upon it shoulders came some distinguishing characteristics that set this creation apart from the animals on this earth and the other parts of creation. Among the most prominent distinguishing features of human beings are the following:

(1) A sound, natural disposition that is ready and capable to be directed to the belief in Allah alone as the object of worship;

(2) An ability to comprehend and understand matters via the intelligence and mind that Allah has bestowed on humans[1];

(3) A free will to decide between the path of goodness or the path of evil, as well as a limited free will to enact that choice that he has made;

(4) A responsibility for the choices he has made, which is a necessary result of being given free will and ability;[1]

---

[1] It can be argued that one aspect that distinguishes humans from other living creatures is the mind—and this is an aspect that the theories of materialism or evolution cannot possibly explain. Cf., T. H. Janabi, *Clinging to a Myth: The Story Behind Evolution* (Burr Ridge, IL: American Trust Publications, 2001), pp. 82-84.

(5) These are all in addition to the fact mentioned earlier that all of the resources of the creation have been subjugated to his use.

Given all of these special characteristics, the human should realize that he has a special and noble purpose and goal in this life. Analogous to the arguments given about the wisdom behind the creation of the cosmos, the creation of humans and the special characteristics that humans possess should make each human realize that the Creator is too wise and lofty to create him simply for sport. "Did you think that We had created you in play (without any purpose), and that you would not be brought back to Us?" (23:115).

Indeed, even more than that, the great Creator who created all the cosmos and the humans—the One who provided even the most detailed needs of the miraculous human anatomy and who is also the Compassionate and Merciful—would not leave humans without guidance and without ordering them and showing them what to do or what not to do. Thus, rhetorically, Allah says, "Does man think that he will be left neglected [without being commanded and also punished or rewarded for the obligatory duties enjoined by his Lord (Allah) on him]?" (75:36).

Hence, the human should realize that his actions in this life have a real ramification to them. In this sense, *nothing* that he does is meaningless or without consequences. His life has purpose here and the Creator is ever aware of every action, thought, intention and movement that he makes.

It is extremely important for the human to realize this point, that he has a purpose in this life. Indeed, this realization may be the first step along a change of life in which one turns to his Great and Wonderful Creator, to submit to Him willfully. Without realizing this fact, there may be no need, meaning or purpose to behaving in a specific manner. If nothing truly matters and if nothing is morally wrong or right, since there is no God or real purpose to existence, it

---

[1] Cf., Anas Karzoon, *Manhaj al-Islaam fi Tazkiyah al-Nafs* (Jeddah: Daar Noor al-Maktabaat, 1997), vol. 1, pp. 20-21.

is expected for people to behave in any fashion they wish. When a person's eyes are open to the reality of this creation, his purpose and role in it, theoretically speaking, there should be a great and profound effect on his life.

Furthermore, as Karzoon noted,

> When a person becomes heedless of his goal for which he was created and the role that he has been given, he becomes busy with other goals... This changes them [that is, such people] from their essential human nature and position by which Allah honored them. Due to this, contradiction and confusion occurs in the make-up of the human. The human is then dragged into two different directions: the direction of the spirit (*rooh*) and the direction of the body.[1]

Karzoon then notes that the only way to make those two aspects compatible is via the teachings of Islam. It is these teachings alone that can properly and in a balanced manner fulfill the needs of both the spirit and the body. Ignoring that purpose and that path is what leads to the kind of society that exists today, wherein a primary goal is the meeting of the desires while greater and more important ethical and moral issues and needs are being ignored.[2]

At this point, it is worthwhile to discuss some other views of humans and human nature, views that clearly and unequivocally contradict the Islamic view of humankind.

The first view is that humans are simply some kind of purposeless, accidental, material being that has appeared without a Creator.[3] The leading existentialists such as Sartre and Camus taught the absurdity or meaningless of life and every action. Others have also expressed this approach to life. Jacques Monod, Noble Prize winning physician who died in 1976, stated,

---

[1] Karzoon, vol. 1, p. 24.
[2] Karzoon, vol. 1, p. 25.
[3] Or via a Creator who has no interest in what the human does.

> Man knows, at last, that he is alone in the indifferent immensity of the universe in which he emerged by chance. He knows now that, like a gypsy, he is marginal to the universe in which he lives: a universe that is deaf to his music and indifferent to his hopes, his suffering, and his crimes.[1]

Steven Weinberg, also a Nobel Prize-winner, stated, "The more we know the universe, the more it appears pointless and strange to us."[2]

The earlier discussion demonstrates how different this view is from the Islamic perspective. At the same time, though, it may be good to note what kind of influence this view of humankind may have on the human psyche and human behavior.

Victor Hugo, the French author, was obviously not a Muslim. However, one does not have to be a Muslim to realize the evil effects of this materialistic view of life, wherein there is no purpose, no Hereafter, no eventual meeting with one's Lord. Hugo was thus able to describe the effects of this materialist, purposeless doctrine on people. He wrote,

> The inclination of people to limit all considerations to the present life is catastrophic. In fact, by convincing man that the material life he has on earth is the noblest aim of existence, and that there is no real purpose after death — by doing this, the troubles of living will loom larger and their cost heavier. Consequently, the concept of afterlife becomes impossible; and pain, a divine law that leads to perfection, turns into a law of despair leading to Hell. The same thing applies to the rest of social affairs... What makes the burden of life light, and the person strong, tolerant, reasonable,

---

[1] Quoted in Abdessalam Yassine, *Winning the Modern World for Islam* (Iowa City, IA: Justice and Spirituality Publishing, Inc., 2000), p. 74.

[2] Quoted in Yassine, p. 75.

patient, brave, courageous and at the same time modest, great and worthy of freedom — is what always seems to be a perfect, eternal life the light of which gleams through the darkness of the present life… The duty of everyone of us is to turn his face to the heavens, and all souls to the Afterlife where true justice is established and every person is judged by his deeds.[1]

This author has had personal experience working in prisons in the United States. Upon asking numerous inmates why they committed their crimes, the response was invariably, "Why not?" The only question to them was whether they could get away with an act and not get caught. There was no question of any responsibility towards a Creator or any sense of purpose in this life. Indeed, one cannot argue much against their way of thinking if one is foolish enough to believe that this existence is purposeless and by mere chance.

In sum, it can be argued that the belief that humans are purposeless and the result of mere material chance encounters seems to be illogical and is potentially very harmful—especially in the long-run (after death) for the human.

A second notion which can have just as devastating affects as the above—and which can be considered a subset of the above—is the notion that humans are simply descended from animals in some evolutionary sense. In this way of thinking, humans are doubly a process of mere materialist elements as well as being directly descended from animals, apes being the closest relative. The Quranic notion concerning the creation of the first human was touched upon earlier. It clearly shows that humans are a distinct creature that God created and were not the result of any kind of evolution or metamorphosis of already existing animals.

---

[1] Quoted in Tabbarah, p. 68.

This approach is best known as Darwinism.[1] What does it mean for a human to consider himself nothing more than an animal—a somewhat higher form of an ape? Can this be used to justify animalistic behavior on the part of humans? Does life become all about survival of the fittest, procreation and domination? There is actually a field of psychology today known as Darwinian psychology or evolutionary psychology in which acts of humans are interpreted exactly in this fashion. Even violent acts of rape are seen as the result of a genetic compulsion to produce babies.[2]

Umar al-Ashqar wrote about Darwinism, "Darwin's principle of the survival of the fittest has destroyed human life, because it has given justification for every oppressor, whether an individual or a government. When the oppressor engages in oppression, confiscation, war and plots, he does not think that he is doing anything wrong— rather, he is following a natural law, according to Darwin's claims, the law of the survival of the fittest. This claim led to the ugliest excesses of colonialism."[3]

Actually, what al-Ashqar described is not some afterthought that came as a result of Darwinistic types of theories. Those people who originally propounded the theories believed in such conclusions. Note the following passage from Mamdani,

> Herbert Spencer wrote in *Social Statics* (1850), "The forces which are working out the great scheme of perfect happiness, taking no account of incidental suffering, exterminate such sections of mankind as stand in their way." This is a train of

---

[1] It is best to avoid a lengthy, detailed discussion of Darwinism from an Islamic perspective. A number of Muslim authors have written on this topic and the interested reader may consult:al-Ashqar, pp.138-156; Janabi, *passim*; Ruqaiyyah Waris Maqsood, *Thinking About God* (Plainfield, IN: American Trust Publications, 1994), pp. 71-89.

[2] A critique of such Darwinian psychology is Anne Innis Dagg, *"Love of Shopping" Is not a Gene: Problems with Darwinian Psychology* (Montreal: Black Rose Books, 2005). The critique is useful but Dagg's own conclusions about life are inconsistent with Islamic teachings, to say the least.

[3] Al-Ashqar, *Belief in Allah*, p. 144.

thought Charles Lyell had pursued twenty years earlier in *Principles of Geology*: if "the most significant and diminutive of species ... have each slaughtered their thousands, why should not we, the lords of creation, do the same?" His student, Charles Darwin, confirmed in *The Descent of Man* (1871) that "at some future period not very distant as measured in centuries, the civilized races of man will almost certainly exterminate and replace throughout the world the savage races." "After Darwin," comments Sven Lindqvist in his survey of European thought on genocide, "it became accepted to shrug your shoulders at genocide. If you were upset, you were just showing your lack of education."[1]

Ignoring the fact that there are many "missing links" and scientific doubts raised against the theory of evolution[2], could this possibly be what this great and grandeur cosmos is all about? Could humans, who have been given so many capabilities above and beyond the animals, be nothing more than animals without any noble purpose or Creator to answer to? Again, as was stated about the materialistic, accidental view, of which this is only a subset, it can be argued that

---

[1] Mahmood Mamdani, *Good Muslim, Bad Muslim: America, the Cold War, and the Roots of Terror* (New York: Pantheon Books, 2004), p. 262.

[2] It is truly amazing how the debate is spreading in the United States over the question of intelligent design, creationism and evolution. Anyone who does not believe in some strong form of evolution seems to be looked upon as dogmatic, backwards and unscientific. The theory is presented to students as if it were above critique or that not critique even exists. Thus, C. P. Martin wrote in *American Scientist*, "It is not that they are aware of the difficulties ... and esteem them of little weight or importance; they never heard of them and are amazed at the bare possibility of the accepted theory being criticized" (quoted in Maqsood, p. 71). The fact is that no honest scientist will call evolution anything more than "the theory of evolution"; it is a theory held by many but certainly not scientific fact. The theory itself has many gaping holds in it as discussed by al-Ashqar, Janabi and Maqsood in the references cited earlier.

this view seems to be completely illogical and potentially very harmful.

In addition to the above views concerning the nature of humans, there are actually some who believe in the Creator and yet they have this notion that humans are inherently evil. At first glance, this belief already seems strange in that God has provided so much for humankind and the rest of the cosmos that it seems inconsistent to then conclude that this most blessed creation has been created as something evil. Nevertheless, this is a belief that is held by many Jews and Christians, in particular.

Concerning the Jewish belief, Karzoon noted that the Talmud teaches that the soul is inherently evil. The Jewish rabbis considered the attainment of virtue to be something very difficult since it goes against the nature of humankind. It was God's plan, they claim, to make humans inherently evil while obliging them to follow a law that would be beyond their ability. Hence, man is in a loss between following his natural, evil inclinations or following the law from God. For that reason, they claim, David was not sinful when he murdered and committed adultery because the real cause for his plight was God Himself.[1] Obviously, if this is a person's perception of the human soul, it must become very easy to allow one's soul to be completely denigrated and abased. If righteousness is beyond reach, what is the use in even trying to achieve it? Indeed, it should be expected that one commits sins and one be angered with God for making a religion that is beyond the capability of humans.

The Islamic view of the human soul is very different—and completely consistent with what one would conclude from pondering over the greatness of the creation of the cosmos. In a hadith quoted earlier, the Prophet Muhammad (peace and blessings of Allah be upon him) himself said, "Every child is born on the *fitrah* (the natural way, the religion of Islam). It is his parents who then make

---

[1] Karzoon, vol. 1, pp. 99-100. Also see the respective references that he refers to in that work.

him into a Jew, Christian or Magian."[1] That is, far from the child being born inherently evil, every child is born upon the true religion. It is only afterwards, the influence of family, society and environment, that an individual becomes influenced to follow paths that are not pure. Additionally, the law that God revealed for humankind is something that is within their means. Allah says in the Quran, "Allah burdens not a person beyond his scope" (2:286), and, furthermore, "Allah puts no burden on any person beyond what He has given him. Allah will grant after hardship, ease" (65:7). Thus, both aspects of the Jewish belief are considered wrong from an Islamic perspective. There is no question that the Jewish belief discussed here seems clearly false and potentially harmful for the well-being of humans.

Christians believe in the concept of the "original sin." This is the belief that the sin that Adam, the first man, committed is passed on through all of his progeny. Hence, it is on the neck of every individual, even the newborn baby. The only way it could be removed—they claim—is by God sending His son as a sacrifice to remove this sin. This belief, especially the last part of it, is obviously completely inconsistent with Islamic monotheism. God does not have a son. He has no equals or anyone who is in any fashion similar to or "related" to Him.

The Islamic belief is that Adam and Eve together did commit a sin, by allowing themselves to be deceived by Satan. However, they both repented to God and God accepted their repentance. That was the end of their sin. There was no means for that sin to be passed on to others. Furthermore, it would be the height of injustice on the part of Allah to hold innocent individuals responsible for the sins of others. Thus, Allah says, "No person earns any (sin) except against himself (only), and no bearer of burdens shall bear the burden of another" (6:164). Allah also says, "And no bearer of burdens shall bear another's burden, and if one heavily

---

[1] Recorded by al-Bukhari and Muslim.

laden calls another to (bear) his load, nothing of it will be lifted even though he be near of kin" (35:18; also see 17:15 and 39:7).

Therefore, the concept of the original sin seems clearly false and is also potentially harmful.[1] It gives a very wrong impression about God and His justice. It also taints the human with the belief that his soul is inherently evil.

It is not by "mere chance" that all of the above other perspectives seem clearly false and potentially harmful. Just like humans are not here by "mere chance," there is only one belief system about humankind that is true, consistent with the cosmos, logical and beneficial. It is, this author contends, the view based on the teachings from God as found in the religion of Islam and explained throughout these pages.

---

[1] It seems to be a false belief even from a Biblical perspective. God does not hold individuals guilty of the sins of others, even if it be their own father. Thus, Ezekiel 18:20 states: "The soul that sinneth, it shall die. The son shall not bear the iniquity of the father, neither shall the father bear the iniquity of the son: the righteousness of the righteous shall be upon him, and the wickedness of the wicked shall be upon him" (*King James Version*). Note that if the idea of the Original Sin falls apart, then virtually all of Christian theology, which centers around Jesus dying on the cross and the significance of that sacrifice, also falls apart.

The Human Being

Already much has been said about the human being but there are still some important aspects that deserve to be touched upon in a chapter of its own.

The Nobility of Humans

Humans are a creation of God. Humans are not divine in any way whatsoever. They do not share any divine qualities with God. This is true for humankind as a whole as well as for each individual human. No human is a literal son or daughter of God. In fact, humans should realize that they are not the greatest or most magnificent of what Allah has created. Allah says, "The creation of the heavens and the earth is indeed greater than the creation of mankind, yet most of mankind know not" (40:57). It should be humbling for a human to reflect upon what a small speck in the mass of God's creation he truly is.

At the same time, though, Allah has blessed mankind in many ways and given them virtues above and beyond much of Allah's creation. Thus, one reads in the Quran, "And indeed We have honored the Children of Adam, and We have carried them on land and sea, and have provided them with lawful good things, and have preferred them above many of those whom We have created with a marked preference" (17:70).

In reality, every human has two very different possible potentials awaiting him. This has been the case since the creation of the first human. When Adam was created, the angels were ordered to bow down to him. These angels are spiritual forces that are always ready to be at the side of humans when they wish to do good deeds. At the same time, there was Satan[1] who vowed to be humankind's enemy and to mislead as many humans as possible. Thus, the two potentials were established.

---

[1] Satan, according to Islamic beliefs, was not a "fallen angel." Angels would never "fall" or become anything like Satan. Such goes against the very nature of the angels. Satan is from another class of creatures known as the Jinn.

Humans are free to ascend to the highest of heights or to descent to the lowest of lows. These two different choices for humankind are described in various places in the Quran. Allah says, "Verily, We created man of the best stature (mould), Then We reduced him to the lowest of the low, Save those who believe and do righteous deeds, then they shall have a reward without end (Paradise)" (95:4-6). Allah also says, "Verily, those who disbelieve from among the people of the Scripture and polytheists will abide in the Fire of Hell. They are the worst of creatures. Verily, those who believe and do righteous good deeds, they are the best of creatures" (98:6-7).

From these two sets of verses, the key is clear: belief and actions. It is by proper belief and righteous actions that one fulfills his purpose in this life and fulfills his greatest potential. Allah describes the purpose of this creation in the verse, "And I (Allah) created not the jinn and humans except they should worship Me (Alone)" (51:56).

Indeed, the goal of life is to worship and please Allah—thus, to receive His pleasure in return. Some people seem to be not attracted by this goal. They seem to think that there is something more that they can forge for themselves. However, such could not be further from the truth. In fact, Allah has described the most noble of creation as His slaves and servants, demonstrating that there is no way of life or being that is more noble and elevated than that of being a true servant of Allah. This is the foremost praise that Allah has bestowed on any of the creation. Allah has said about the angels, for example, "To Him belongs whosoever is in the heavens and on earth. And those who are near Him (i.e. the angels) are not too proud to worship Him, nor are they weary (of His worship). They (i.e. the angels) glorify His Praises night and day, (and) they never slacken (to do so)" (21:19-20).

Such is, along with the angels, the case for the noblest among humankind. God says, "The Messiah will never be proud to reject to be a slave to Allah, nor the angels who are near (to Allah).

And whosoever rejects His worship and is proud, then He will gather them all together unto Himself" (4:172). Indeed, only the most ignorant of people could refuse to submit and be a servant of the Great, Glorious and Magnificent Creator and God.

The Prophet Muhammad (peace and blessings of Allah be upon him) said, "Do not extol me like the Christians extolled the son of Mary. I am His slave-servant, so say, 'Slave of Allah and His Messenger.'"[1]

To be a true servant of God is the ultimate goal for humankind. There can be no greater goal. In fact, this is the only goal that can bring true solace to the soul of humans because this is the goal that is recognized deep within the person's soul. As noted earlier, this wanting to know and worship one's Lord is something deep within the natural make-up of mankind. Without finding this reality, man can never find true happiness.

Furthermore, the most exalted, noble, and honored a human can be is by worshipping Allah. There is nothing greater or nobler than that. That is the maximum potential. This is something that should be clear to every human. The more he moves to that goal, the happier he should become and the more honor he should feel by submitting himself to the only true God and Lord. When he realizes this fact, his efforts should be exerted to maximize this potential.

Actually, when a person realizes that he has only one, clear goal, the effects upon his soul are profound. He need not chase after an endless array of goals, never being able to satisfy or achieve any of them completely. (Indeed, many times people's goals are contradictory and they can never achieve all of them.) His energies need not be exhausted trying to serve a myriad of goals. When he has one goal and one goal alone, he can easily gauge whether he is moving towards achieving that goal or not. He can put all of his energy and thought into working towards that one ultimate goal. He can be certain about his goal and his path will be clear. Hence, he has no reason to be filled with doubt or confusion. As he moves closer

---

[1] Recorded by al-Bukhari.

and closer to that one ultimate goal, he can experience true joy and contentment. Allah has described the state of he who recognizes and seeks the true worship of only one God as opposed to those who seek after many goals and gods: "Allah puts forth a similitude: a (slave) man belonging to many partners (like those who worship others along with Allah) disputing with one another, and a (slave) man belonging entirely to one master, (like those who worship Allah Alone). Are those two equal in comparison? All the praises and thanks be to Allah! But most of them know not" (39:29).

Note that although this is the ultimate purpose for humankind, Allah is actually not in need of human worship. Allah has said, "And whoever disbelieves [then he is a disbeliever of Allah] and Allah stands not in need of any of the humankind or jinn" (3:97). Another verse reads, "And Moses said, 'If you disbelieve, you and all on earth together, then verily, Allah is Rich (Free of all wants), Owner of all Praise'" (14.8).

If this is the case, who then actually benefits from the worship of Allah? It is actually the human who chooses to worship who benefits from the act of worship. He has benefited by purifying his soul, bring tranquility to his heart and, most importantly, by having the correct relationship with God. Allah reminds humankind of this point in numerous places in the Quran. For example, Allah says, "And whosoever strives, he strives only for himself. Verily, Allah is free of all wants from all that exists" (29:6). Another example is the verse, "Whoever gives thanks, he gives thanks for (the good of) his ownself. And whoever is unthankful, then verily, Allah is All-Rich (Free of all wants), Worthy of all praise" (31:12). A final example is, "Whoever goes right, then he goes right only for the benefit of his ownself. And whoever goes astray, then he goes astray to his own loss. No one laden with burdens can bear another's burden. And We never punish until We have sent a Messenger (to give warning)" (17:15).

The Wisdom Behind the Creation of Humans

If the ultimate purpose of humankind is to worship Allah alone and yet Allah does not benefit from such worship, then one may rightly ask: What exactly is the wisdom behind the creation of humans?[1] There is definitely a wisdom behind the creation of humans since, as discussed earlier, Allah has made it clear that He has not created purposeless, in sport, in jest or anything of that nature. Hence, in everything He creates there is wisdom—and He is the All-Wise, the All-Knowing. When the angels asked Allah why He was placing this new creature on the earth, Allah's reply to them was that He had knowledge that they did not.[2]

However, as was the case with pondering over the creation of the heavens and the earth, one can come to some conclusions that may be partial answers to this particular question.

First, one can see that humans are unique beings, especially given their ability to worship Allah, to exercise free will and to use their minds. Allah has created a being that can, as described earlier, rise to the greatest levels of creation or lower himself to the lowest abyss. This creation points to not only the existence of a creator—as a

---

[1] As far as this author is aware of, there is no clear text in the Quran or the Sunnah explicitly stating the answer to this question, as opposed to the question of the purpose of humankind. One knows that Allah acts on the basis of wisdom but, obviously, it is not necessary that such wisdom always be apparent to humans. In fact, ibn Abi al-Izz wrote, "It is difficult or impossible for man to understand the wisdom that lies behind Allah's creation or His command" (*op cit.*, p. 41). Later, he also makes the following important point: "If the wisdom of Allah is hidden from us and is not known to us, that does not mean that no purpose or reason underlies the creation or action. Do you not see that the wisdom behind Allah's creation of snakes, scorpions, mice and insects is unknown to us? All we know about these things is that they are harmful. But this does not mean that Allah did not create them or that there is no purpose in Allah's creating them, for ignorance of a matter is not proof of its non-existence" (p. 209). Thus, the above answer is what this author has been able to derive as a possible response to this question.

[2] "And (remember) when your Lord said to the angels, 'Verily, I am going to place (mankind) generations after generations on earth.' They said, 'Will You place therein those who will make mischief therein and shed blood, while we glorify You with praises and thanks and sanctify You.' He (Allah) said, 'I know that which you do not know'" (Quran 2:30).

creation of this nature could not simply come about by chance nor have any other creatures supposedly evolved to such a state—but to the greatness and the amazing knowledge of the Creator. This in itself is a very important aspect and humans should reflect upon it as, once again, humans cannot escape the fact that they have a Creator and Lord.

Second, the existence of humans which have the ability to do good or evil manifests many of Allah's attributes that are not manifested simply through the creation of the heavens and the earth. Yes, even the existence of "relative evil" is a positive thing.[1] Via the existence of such "evil" Allah's beautiful attributes of forgiveness, mercy, patience and appreciation of deeds are manifested. In addition, His attributes of being just, being able to punish and having power over all creatures are also manifested through deeds that humans often suffer from and wonder why or how God could have allowed them to occur. There is nothing without a purpose and wisdom and in the long-run the individual may realize what great good was brought about by such deeds.

Third, Allah's eternal reward for those who believe and do good demonstrate how loving and compassionate He truly is. He will have His devoted worshippers, who recognized, accepted and fulfilled their purpose in this life, in a state of perpetual felicity, manifesting Allah's greatness in giving and rewarding. On the other hand, the fate of those who willingly choose to ignore all the signs around them and refuse to worship or submit to God will demonstrate Allah's power and ability to judge with complete and true justice.

The Essential Equality of All Humans in Islam

The teachings of Islam are emphatic on a point that modern societies are still trying to grapple with. This is the essential equality

---

[1] Relative evil refers to something that seems to be evil on the surface but which has, in reality, a greater purpose and benefit to it. Perhaps the greatest evil one can imagine is Satan yet in the creation of Satan there is much wisdom and benefit for humankind. Ibn al-Qayyim has written at length on this issue and his writings may be found in English in Umar al-Ashqar, *The World of the Jinn and Devils* (Boulder, CO: Al-Basheer Company for Publications and Translations, 1998), pp. 225-243.

of all humans. All humans are creatures of Allah and each and everyone of them has the ability to soar to the greatest heights of being a human by worshipping and submitting to Allah. As such, there is no distinction between any of them as humans—it is only the choices that humans make that will distinguish them in the sight of Allah, the Law and other members of the community. However, race, color or nationality have no role to play in this whatsoever.

Allah says, "O mankind! We have created you from a male and a female, and made you into nations and tribes, that you may know one another. Verily, the most honorable of you with Allah is that (believer) who has piety. Verily, Allah is All-Knowing, All-Aware" (49:13). The Prophet (peace and blessings of Allah be upon him) made that Quranic teaching most explicit when he stated in front of one of the largest gatherings he had ever assembled, "O people, verily your Lord is One and your [original] father is one. Certainly, there is no virtue in an Arab over a non-Arab or a non-Arab over an Arab. Similarly, there is no virtue in a light-skinned person over a dark-skinned person or a dark-skinned person over a light-skinned person. Only by piety [does one become more virtuous over another]. Have I indeed conveyed to you the message?"[1]

Such discrimination and racism that one still finds in modern times existed before the time of the Prophet (peace and blessings of Allah be upon him) and he eradicated their traces. One time he stated, "Allah has removed from you the blemishes of the days of Ignorance and the boasting about one's lineage. In fact, there is no one but a pious believing person or a wretched evildoer. All humans are descended from Adam and Adam was created from clay."[2]

Adam was created from clay and everyone is descended from that one creature. The silliness of all the racism that exists can be seen in the fact that the differences in the colors of humankind can be

---

[1] Recorded by Ahmad.

[2] Recorded by al-Tirmidhi. Authenticated by al-Albaani. See Muhammad Naasir al-Deen al-Albaani, *Saheeh al-Jaami al-Sagheer* (Beirut: al-Maktab al-Islaami, 1988),, vol. 2, p. 963.

attributed to Adam's origin. The Prophet (peace and blessings of Allah be upon him) stated, "Allah created Adam from a handful which He gathered from throughout the earth. Thus, the descendants of Adam vary as the earth varies: some are red, some are white, some are black, and some are of colors in between, some are easy-going, some are difficult, some are evil and some are good."[1]

Instead of being causes of division among humankind, the variations in people are meant to be signs of the greatness of the Creator. Allah says, "And among His Signs is the creation of the heavens and the earth, and the difference of your languages and colors. Verily, in that are indeed signs for men of sound knowledge" (30:22).

Thus, the door to be a true worshipper of Allah is open to everyone, regardless of race, nationality and so forth. In fact, it is only via such worship of Allah that one becomes deserving of honor and dignity and one becomes full of virtues. This is a tenet of Islam that has been practiced throughout its history.[2]

On this point, the famed historian Arnold Toynbee wrote, "The extinction of race consciousness as between Muslims is one of the outstanding achievements of Islam, and in the contemporary world there is, as it happens, a crying need for the propagation of this Islamic virtue…"[3]

This essential equality of humans covers both males and females—regardless of what propaganda one may hear about Islam.[4] As a spiritual being and one worthy of worshipping Allah, there is no

---

[1] Recorded by Ahmad, Abu Dawood, al-Tirmidhi and others. Authenticated by al-Albaani. See *Saheeh al-Jaami al-Sagheer*, vol. 1, p. 362.

[2] This is not to deny that there may be racism among Muslims—although it has never reached the stage it has in the "modern, civilized West." Such racism is the result of ignorance or a lack of piety. It has never, though, been the case that any form of racism has been sanctioned by the religion itself, as has been the case with other religions.

[3] Quoted in *Islam—The First & Final Religion* (Karachi, Pakistan: Begum Aisha Bawany Waqf, 1978), p. 73.

[4] Much of what one may hear concerning women in Islam is either entirely false or concerning cultural matters that fly in the face of Islamic teachings. As for the latter, Muslim scholars themselves have worked to try to remedy the situation.

difference between a man and a woman.[1] Both of them are equal before God.

Allah says, "Whoever works righteousness, whether male or female, while he (or she) is a true believer verily, to him (or her) We will give a good life, and We shall pay them certainly a reward in proportion to the best of what they used to do [i.e., Paradise in the Hereafter]" (16:97). Allah also says, "The believers, men and women, are supporters of one another, they enjoin what is good, and forbid evil; they establish the prayers, and give the alms, and obey Allah and His Messenger. Allah will have His Mercy on them. Surely Allah is All-Mighty, All-Wise" (9:71). As a final example, God states, "Verily, those who submit to Allah men and women, the believers men and women, the men and the women who are obedient (to Allah), the men and women who are truthful, the men and the women who are patient, the men and the women who are humble, the men and the women who give charity, the men and the women who observe fasts, the men and the women who guard their chastity and the men and the women who remember Allah much with their hearts and tongues Allah has prepared for them forgiveness and a great reward (i.e. Paradise)" (33:35).

It is well-known that Islam gave women many rights that women did not achieve in the West until recently, such as the right to own property and handle their own business affairs.[2] However, there are actually much more important issues. Every ideology, religion or culture values some matters above and beyond others. As is clear from this section, the most important quality in Islam is piety and dutifulness to Allah. Perhaps the second most valued quality in Islam

---

[1] In fact, in Islamic belief, it was both Adam and Eve who committed the original sin together, both repented to Allah and both were forgiven by Allah.

[2] Annie Besant writing around 1932 stated, "I often think that women is more free in Islam than in Christianity… In Al-Quran the law about woman is more just and liberal. It is only in the last twenty years that Christian England has recognized the right of women to property, while Islam has allowed this right from all times…" Quoted in *Islam—The First and Final Religion*, pp. 91-92. See the remainder of the quotes there on this topic, pp. 91-93.

is knowledge of the religion. On both of these issues, women are completely equal to men. Throughout the history of Islam, women have been known and respected for their piety and their knowledge. On the other hand, Islam does not say that a person's value is measured by how beautiful one's face is, how sexy one's body can be, how fast one can run in sports, how well one can sing, dance or act. These are ludicrous criteria of a person's worth from the Islamic perspective—although it seems to be much of what "modern civilization" cares about. In sum, according to the things that have the greatest value in this life—piety and religious knowledge—women are exactly equal to men and this is a most important statement of equality given the Islamic criteria.

Human Rights and Islamic Law

Related to the dignity of humans is the question of "human rights." It is not unusual to read Western writers claiming that the concept of human rights is a Western invention. For example, Ann Mayer writes, "Concepts of human rights are just one part of a cluster of institutions transplanted since the nineteenth century from the West."[1] Again, J. Donnelly wrote,

> Most non-western cultural and political traditions
> lack not only the practice of human rights but the
> very concept. As a matter of historical fact, the
> concept of human rights is an artifact of modern
> western civilization.[2]

In reality, though, all legal codes have given necessary rights to humans. In fact, one could argue that such is most true of Islam, which guaranteed numerous rights to all of humankind. Islam is a religion of justice, rights and rule of law and it safeguarded these rights of humans some fourteen hundred years ago.

---

[1] Ann Elizabeth Mayer, *Islam and Human Rights* (Boulder, CO: Westview Press, 1999), p. 9.

[2] J. Donnelly, "Human Rights and Dignity: An Analytic Critique of Non-Western Human Rights Conceptions" *American Political Science Review* (1982, 76), p. 303.

For this reason, when Muslim scholars studied the Universal Declaration of Human Rights (UDHR)[1], they found that the vast majority of the declaration was already affirmed and put into practice by the religion of Islam.[2] Thus, if one takes a cursory look at some human rights listed in the UDHR, it can be easily shown that such rights have been affirmed and protected by Islam. To take some of the articles at random, Article 3 reads, "Everyone has the right to life, liberty and the security of person" and Article 7 reads, "All are equal before the law and are entitled without any discrimination to equal protection of the law. All are entitled to equal protection against any discrimination in violation of this Declaration and against any incitement to such discrimination." One can say such rights are not only protected in Islamic Law but that it forms part of the goals of the Law itself to protect rights of this nature.

To this day, there is dispute over what should be considered the fundamental human rights. There is, of course, a very important question that secular human rights advocates have historically had difficulties answering: On what basis can one claim that something is a fundamental human right? Do humans truly have the knowledge and ability to determine what are fundamental human rights? Shouldn't the determining of such fundamental human rights be related to knowledge of the very essence and souls of humans while it must be admitted that humans have had very little success in penetrating the vast mysteries of the human soul?

The Islamic answer to these types of question is quite simple: It is the Creator who has the knowledge and authority to determine what is a fundamental human right and no one else. Only God can determine in an unbiased manner and in a manner that is most consistent with human nature, as well as individual and societal

---

[1] In reality, this UN document never became legally binding. Hence, new conventions were proposed and adopted, such as the Convention on Civil and Political Rights.

[2] There were a small number of articles that the Muslim scholars objected to as being in contradiction with specific Islamic laws. For details on this issue, see Sulieman al-Hageel, *Human Rights in Islam and a Refutation of the Misconceived Allegations Associated with These Rights* (Supreme Council for Islamic Affairs, 2001), pp. 70-77.

needs, what must be considered the fundamental rights of humans. To leave such a grave matter solely to human reasoning—which has differed over the rights and have obviously changed their minds over time as to what such rights should be[1]—and distanced from the revelation from God is fraught with danger. Thus, God says in the Quran, "And if the truth had been in accordance with their desires, verily, the heavens and the earth, and whosoever is therein would have been corrupted" (23:71).

Incidentally, there is yet another important difference between the Islamic view of human rights and any secular view of human rights. Muslims see the human rights sanctioned by Islam as God-given rights that cannot be violated in any way. They are not political weapons that are defended only when politically expedient and otherwise simply ignored. In obedience to God, a Muslim must respect the rights of others as given by the religion of Islam. This has been manifested in the behavior of Muslims throughout their history. Even when war had to be resorted to, Muslims had very strict guidelines that they had to abide by and they were known to abide by them. One can find no example of Muslim armies perpetuating the kind of violence and slaughter that took place at the hands of the Crusaders when they entered Jerusalem. Similarly, this author is fairly certain that Muslims never committed the kinds of atrocities that were committed recently at Abu Ghraib, although they were committed—and sometimes even defended—by a people who claim to believe in human rights, freedom, democracy and so forth.

Finally, when humans discuss and determine human rights, the scope must be very limited. They can only discuss worldly aspects. In this way, they are neglecting the most important right of a human—a right that can only be granted by Allah. To know this right, one has to turn to revelation and the prophets. The Prophet Muhammad (peace and blessings of Allah be upon him) explained

---

[1] In the Beijing Conference on Women, some groups were pushing for certain sexual freedoms, such as lesbianism, as fundamental human rights. Such a suggestion would have been unthinkable just some fifty years ago.

this right when he was speaking to one of his companions and he said, "Do you know what the right of Allah upon His servants is?" The companion replied, "Allah and His Messenger know best." The Prophet (peace and blessings of Allah be upon him) then said, "The right of Allah upon His servants is that He is worshipped alone and no partner is ascribed to Him." Then after a while he asked his companion, "Do you know what the right of the servants is upon Allah if they adhere to that?" He replied, "Allah and His Messenger know best." The Prophet (peace and blessings of Allah be upon him) then told him, "The right of the servants upon Allah is that He will not punish them."[1]

---

[1] Recorded by al-Bukhari and Muslim.

Religion

Now that the creation and humans have been discussed in detail, it is time to discuss the need for religion itself. In addition, the basis on which a religion is to be accepted will also be discussed.

Human's Need for Religion

The world has entered into a very materialistic stage. It seemed that science had conquered nature and there was no need for religion, myths and superstitions of earlier times. Hence, Nietzsche would have the audacity to proclaim, "God is dead."

However, religion has not gone away. This has even led scientists to try to determine why religion and the belief in God simply will not go away. In fact, a recently published book is entitled, *Why God Won't Go Away: Brain Science & the Biology of Belief.*[1]

Not only has religion not gone away but in recent times there has been a resurgence in religion throughout the world. There has not only been a resurgence in religion itself but a resurgence in fundamentalist religion—a fact that has worried many a secularist.

From the texts of the Quran and Sunnah, it is clear that "religion" is something natural and innate in humans. Allah created humans with a natural disposition that longs to know God and worship Him. Allah says, "So set you (O Muhammad) your face towards the religion of pure Islaamic Monotheism, with which He has created mankind. No change let there be in the Religion of Allah, that is the straight religion, but most of men know not" (30:30). Allah also describes an event that took place in the life of every human—but his "life" before he became a being in this physical world and which must exist somewhere deep in his conscience. Allah says, "And (remember) when your Lord brought forth from the Children of Adam, from their loins, their seed (or from Adam's loin his offspring) and made them testify as to themselves (saying), 'Am I not your Lord?' They said, 'Yes! We testify,' lest you should say on

---

[1] Andrew Newberg, Eugene D'Aquili and Vince Rause, *Why God Won't Go Away: Brain Science & the Biology of Belief* (New York: Ballantine Books, 2001).

the Day of Resurrection, 'Verily, we have been unaware of this'"
(7:172).

The Prophet (peace and blessings of Allah be upon him) also said, "Behold, my Lord commanded me that I should teach you that which you do not know and which He has taught me today... [God has stated] 'I have created My servants all having a natural inclination to the worship of Allah. But the devils come to them and turn them away from their [true] religion. And he makes unlawful what I declared lawful for them and he commands them to ascribe partners with Me for which no authority has been sent down.'"[1]

This quote clarifies that there are evil forces that may try to hide, conceal or distort this natural inclination in humans but they can never truly kill what is so deeply rooted in a person's soul.[2] Furthermore, if they can kill this natural tendency in some humans, they will not be able to kill it in all humans. Hence, at least some humans, if not the majority, will always recognize God and that with God comes a religion—a set of beliefs and practices related to God. Thus, it is not by coincidence that virtually every people have had some form of religion and some concrete belief in the Ultimate Being or God.

What the materialists of this world will never be able to deny is that humans are made up of a physical component and a non-

---

[1] Recorded by Muslim.

[2] In fact, even though they may try to deny belief in and responsibility to God, every once in a while the truth that is in the soul—and the recognition of there being only one God and Creator—shines forth. This is especially true when the human is faced with disaster and knows that he has turn to the source of the whole creation. Unfortunately, once God relieves the human of his distress, he usually reverts to his old ways and once again forgets about God. This phenomenon is described in a number of places in the Quran. For example, Allah says, "He it is Who enables you to travel through land and sea, till when you are in the ships and they sail with them with a favorable wind, and they are glad therein, then comes a stormy wind and the waves come to them from all sides, and they think that they are encircled therein, they invoke Allah, making their Faith pure for Him Alone, saying: 'If You (Allah) deliver us from this, we shall truly be of the grateful'" (10:22).

physical component, called the soul or spiritual side of humans.[1] Materialists—and material comforts—can only touch upon the physical side of a human. They can do nothing to assist the vast spiritual side of humans, leaving a great void in the psyche of a human. When humans experience this vacuum, they realize that something is wrong. They seek something to fill this void. Although they may turn to more material things or different types of material things (alcoholism, drugs), such things will never truly fill that void in their lives.

If they can get above all of the materialistic propaganda around them today, they realize that it is God and religion that is missing from their lives and from their hearts. Unfortunately, they may be again deceived into then following some of the false religions that exist today, ever seeking that thing that the soul is constantly yearning for. But many are guided to the true path by God and their souls find what they have been truly seeking since birth. Many make this realization and act upon it, changing their lives forever.

The famed Islamic scholar Ibn Taimiyyah once wrote,

---

[1] Although many may not deny the existence of the soul, it seems that they go out of their way to avoid using or referring to this term. The psychiatrist and physician M. Scott Peck shows that it is more than coincidence that the word "soul" is missing from the vocabulary of many researchers today. In *Denial of the Soul*, he wrote, "The word 'soul' is probably in the vocabulary of every second-grader… Then why is it that [it] is not in the professional lexicon of psychiatrists, other mental health workers, students of the mind, and physicians in general? There are two reasons. One is that the concept of God is inherent in the concept of soul, and 'God talk' is virtually off-limits within these relatively secular professions. Religious though individuals in these professions might be personally, they would not want to offend their secular colleagues. Nor, for that matter, would they care to lose their jobs. The fact is that to speak of God or the soul in their professional gatherings would be politically incorrect. The other reason is that these professionals properly have a test for intellectual rigor, and the soul is something that cannot be completely defined… Yet this impossibility of adequate definition is not the primary stumbling block. Psychiatrists have no difficulty including 'light,' 'love,' and 'consciousness' in their professional vocabulary. Their primary problem with the 'soul word' is the blatancy of its connection to God." M. Scott Peck, *Denial of the Soul: Spiritual and Medical Perspectives on Euthanasia and Morality* (New York: Harmony Books, 1997), pp. 129-130.

The heart can only become sound, achieve success, take pleasure, be satisfied, experience enjoyment, become pleased, attain serenity and calmness through the *'ibaadah* [worship] of its Lord, having love of Him and turning to Him (in repentance). Even if it were to attain every type of pleasure from creation, it will not acquire serenity and tranquility. This is because the heart possesses an intrinsic need for its Lord, since He is its deity, love and pursuit and with Allah the heart achieves joy, pleasure, delight, amenity, serenity and tranquility.[1]

Ibn Taimiyyah's statement is supported by verses of the Quran. For example, Allah says, "Those who believe, and whose hearts find rest in the remembrance of Allah, verily, in the remembrance of Allah do hearts find rest" (13:28). Allah also says, "O you who believe! Answer Allah and (His) Messenger when he calls you to that which will give you life" (8:24). It is the real life—the only life that is worthy of living—that Allah and His Messenger are calling each and every individual to. It is the real life and salvation for the heart as it frees it from being enslaved to desires, lusts and doubts. It is the real life for the mind and it rescues it from ignorance, doubt and confusion. It is the real life for the human himself as it frees him from servitude and slavery to other humans and ideologies. It frees him to worship and serve Allah alone, the ultimate goal that his own self recognizes and yearns for. This is the source of his honor and dignity, the purpose for which he has been created. In the end, it is the real life of eternal bliss and happiness, in Paradise, being pleased with the Lord and the Lord being pleased with the servant.

(What has been stressed here is the individual's need to know Allah and religion. While discussing the need for prophets, the need for religion from a societal perspective will be discussed.)

---

[1] [Ahmad ibn Taimiyyah,] *Ibn Taymiyyah's Essay on Servitude* (Birmingham, United Kingdom: al-Hidaayah Publishing and Distribution, 1999), p. 121.

The Parameters of the True Religion

Mere reflection on the history of humans demonstrates that humans have a desire to have religion. Yet there are many religions and each is presenting itself as the "true religion" that will bring solace to the individual. Thus, in this section, the author would like to present what he feels are the four parameters by which one may distinguish the true religion.

The first parameter is that the religion must have God as its original source. No one can know the details about God except God. He is above and beyond the realm of human experience. More importantly, no one knows how He should be worshipped except Him. Although humans are able to come to many sound conclusions about God, no human could logically claim that he has somehow—independent of revelation from God—discovered the way in which God should be worshipped and the way that is pleasing to God. Thus, if the ultimate goal in one's heart is to truly please and worship God as He should be worshipped, then one has no alternative but to turn to Him for guidance and direction. (Furthermore, no one can know the details of the human soul except for its Creator.)

Thus, based on this first premise, any man-made religion is not a logical alternative. No matter how hard humans may try, they cannot authoritatively speak about how God is supposed to be worshipped.

As a corollary to or further explanation of this parameter, the beliefs and the teachings of the religion must originate with God. This parameter does not mean that one time God played a role in the formation of the religion. No, this parameter means that the entire scope of the religious teachings come from God. There are some religions that may have originated from God but, afterwards, their adherents felt free to rely upon human reasoning to adjust, modify or alter the religion. In the process, they have actually created a new religion, different from that which God had revealed. This, once again, completely defeats the purpose. What God revealed does not need any improvement or changes from humankind. Any such change or alteration means a deviation away from what God revealed. Thus, any change or alteration will only take humankind away from the true and proper way of worshipping God. Furthermore, God is more than capable of revealing a perfect revelation for any time or circumstance. If there were any need to alter or change any of God's laws, the authority for that also rests only with God. In other words, God is free to change some of His laws due to His wisdom and knowledge, for example, out of mercy or as a form of punishment upon His servants. He may do this by sending a new revelation or even by sending a new prophet. With that, there is no logical problem. But there is a grave problem when humans take it upon themselves to "fix" God's revelation.

The violation of this first parameter has been a common practice. It seems that humans want to relegate to themselves ultimate authority. However, it must be understood that this contradicts the very essence of submitting to and worshipping God. One is no longer submitting to and obeying God alone. One is now submitting to God, human leaders and perhaps even one's own opinions as well. This is the antithesis of pure and devoted worship of God.

Thus, the first parameter states that the religion originates with God. However, this is not sufficient. The second parameter is that the teachings from God must be preserved in their original form. The logic behind this point should be obvious. If the original revelation came from God but was then later tampered and distorted by humans, one now has a mixture of God's religion and human interpolation. This is no longer God's pure religion. Although this may seem like an obvious premise, it is amazing to see many people who have not even considered this point, blindly following scriptures or teachings that cannot be historically authenticated.

The third parameter is that the religion is not abrogated or superseded by a later form of the religion. In other words, God may reveal more than one revelation or send more than one prophet, with the latter repealing or superseding the earlier. Under such circumstances, if one is truly submitting to God, one does not have the right to choose to follow an abrogated teaching and neglect the teaching that God is now demanding to be followed. Again, this would violate the principle of submitting to God and would arrogate to the individual the right to choose what he willed to follow instead of what Allah has decreed.

The above three parameters are straightforward and obvious. In this author's opinion, though, there is also a fourth parameter. The fourth parameter is that the basic beliefs of the religion have to be something fathomable by humans and not repugnant to human nature. It is inconceivable that the same God who created such order and gave humans the ability to understand and derive lessons from what is around them would then ask of them to believe in matters that are completely unfathomable to them and inconsistent with what the soul can accept as truth.

The Situation of the Previous Religions

In this section, the author would like to discuss the plight of Judaism, Christianity and Islam within the framework of the above four parameters.[1]

The first parameter, again, is that the religion must have its original source with God. Again, this means that the beliefs and teachings of the religion must originate with God, without any claim that humans have a right to change or alter them in any way.

In the Quran, Allah condemns the practice of the Jews and Christians who allowed their rabbis and priests to lay down new teachings or laws in contravention of God's revelation. Allah says, "They [the Jews and Christians] took their rabbis and their monks to be their lords besides Allah [by obeying them in things which they made lawful or unlawful according to their own desires without being ordered by Allah], and (they also took as their Lord) Messiah, son of Mary, while they were commanded to worship none but One God, none has the right to be worshipped but He. Praise and glory be to

---

[1] Again, the emphasis here will be on these three religions but a similar study could be carried out for all the various religions of the world.

Him, (far above is He) from having the partners they associate (with Him)" (9:31).

The most widespread form of Judaism known today is called Rabbinical Judaism. This is due to the role that the rabbis, humans, play in forming laws and being an authority in the religion. Much of the religion is based on the Talmud,[1] a work compiled of Jewish writings many centuries after the Exodus but supposedly based on the oral tradition passed on from the time of Moses. For traditional Judaism, it is a must to believe in the Talmud. Rabbi Aaron Parry explains the place of the Talmud in the following passage,

> For Jews, belief in the oral tradition that is the Talmud is an essential cornerstone of faith… Jews believe that virtually nothing of the Torah can be properly understood without the Talmud, a point made clear in the following story from the Talmud:
> A prospective convert goes first to the great sage Shammai and asks the venerable leader how many "Torahs" do the Jews have. He answers two—the Written Law and the Oral Law. The man states that he wishes to convert even though he doesn't believe in the Oral Code. Shammai, indignant over such unheard of conditions, summarily dismisses the fellow and shows him the door.
> …Denying the origins of the oral Torah constitutes denying the origins of the written text as well… When it comes to the Talmud, it's important to understand that for Moses, who heard God's revelations, there was no "doubt." Therefore, traditional Jewish practice also holds that the Talmud represents God's divine will and instruction. We trust in the power of the sages of

---

[1] The Talmud is, "An authoritative, influential compilation of rabbinic traditions and discussions about Jewish life and law." *Larousse Dictionary of Beliefs and Religions* (Edinburgh: Larousse, 1995), p. 513.

each generation, and their followers, to accurately transmit it.[1]

According to *The Dictionary of the Bible*, "[T]he Talmud is considered, at least by orthodox Jews, as the highest authority on all matters of faith…It is, therefore, hardly an exaggeration to say that the Talmud is of equal authority with Scripture in orthodox Judaism."[2] This equality between Scripture and something which is obviously the work of humans, as the above story from the Rabbi Shammai which forms part of the Talmud demonstrates, is illogical.

In fact, according to Karzoon, in the Talmud it states that there was a dispute between God and the Jewish scholars. After a lengthy debate with no resolution, they decided to refer the matter to one of the rabbis. After his decision, God was forced to admit that He was mistaken.[3] Thus, God is not even perfect with respect to His knowledge. If Jews believe this, it would not be surprising to find Jews turning away from the revelation from God for perhaps "better sources of knowledge". Thus, even though the revelation to Moses was originally from God, the Jewish faith has allowed humans to step in and overrule such revelation.

The story of Christianity is even more dramatic. Many call today's Christianity "Pauline Christianity." This is due to the influence that Paul had in forming the beliefs of the Christian Church. It must be noted that there is no evidence that Paul was ever a messenger from God. He was not even one of Jesus' apostles. Instead, he was someone who was persecuting Christians until he saw a vision that led to his conversion to Christianity. When Paul began to spread his new version of Christianity, the leaders of the Church in Jerusalem, including Jesus' own brother James, opposed him.[4]

---

[1] Rabbi Aaron Parry, *The Complete Idiot's Guide to the Talmud* (New York, NY: Alpha Books, 2004), pp. 9-10.

[2] Quoted in M. M. Al-Azami, *The History of the Quranic Text from Revelation to Compilation: A Comparative Study with the Old and New Testaments* (Leicester, United Kingdom: UK Islamic Academy, 2003), p. 250.

[3] Cf., Karzoon, vol. 1, p. 97.

[4] According to the teachings of the New Testament, James was Jesus' brother.

Frederick Grant noted, "To this day it remains clear that both Paul, the Greek, and Matthew, the Jewish missionary, had their own independent perspectives which completely differed from the other concerning the actions and teachings of Jesus."[1] Even given such facts, he was able to establish a new interpretation of the teachings of Jesus—an interpretation that cannot be traced to Jesus nor, by default, to God.[2] The most egregious of such beliefs that he entered into the religion was the belief that true salvation is related to the crucifixion and the shedding of the blood of Jesus.

Thus, the link between the teachings of the religion and God as its source were broken very early in the history of Christianity. Later the Church headed by the Pope appropriated to itself the right to expound new teachings and to declare the truths of the religion. Today, contemporary churches are still following this pattern. Hence, one can find churches completely accepting of homosexuality even

---

[1] Quoted in *Dialogue Between Islam and Christianity: Discussion of Religious Dogma Between Intellectuals from the Two Religions* (Fairfax, VA: Institute of Islamic and Arabic Sciences in America, 1999), p. 38. In fact, Paul virtually boasts about the fact that his teachings cannot be traced back to the teachers of the religion and it all comes to him through the vision that he had received, "But I certify you, brethren, that the gospel which was preached of me is not after man… But when it pleased God, who separated me from my mother's womb, and called me by his grace, To reveal his Son in me, that I might preach him among the heathen; immediately I conferred not with flesh and blood: Neither went I up to Jerusalem to them which were apostles before me; but I went into Arabia, and returned again unto Damascus. Then after three years I went up to Jerusalem to see Peter, and abode with him fifteen days. But other of the apostles saw I none, save James the Lord's brother" (Galatians 1:11 and 1:15-19).

[2] This unique history of Christianity has led people to write books with titles such as *Follow Jesus or Follow Paul?* by Roshan Enam and *The Mythmaker: Paul and the Invention of Christianity* by Hyam Maccoby. Perhaps the most important issue concerning Paul is not the fact that he never met Jesus nor the fact that his teachings led him to disputes with the direct students of Jesus, but the most important issue concerning Paul is whether he was willing to lie to try to promote his beliefs and religion. This doubt concerning Paul is based on Paul's own statement in Romans 3:7: "For if the truth of God hath more abounded through my lie unto his glory; why yet am I also judged as a sinner?" (*King James Version*). Indeed, one can even question whether Paul would be willing to follow God if it went against his conceived notions of truth. Paul himself states, "But though we, or an angel from heaven, preach any other gospel unto you than that which we have preached unto you, let him be accursed" (Galatians 1:8, *King James Version*).

though the teachings of the Bible on this question seem—at least from an outsider's perspective—to be quite clear.

In Islam, though, one finds a very different picture. There is no priesthood in Islam.[1] Every scholar, no matter how great, is simply a human who is prone to error. Hence, any ruling made by anyone must be judged in the light of the Quran and the Sunnah of the Prophet (peace and blessings of Allah be upon him).[2] The Quran and Sunnah have remained the ultimate authority, no one having the right to violate them. This is an agreed upon principle in Islam. In fact, the most respected scholars were not in favor of having their own opinions passed on and were adamant that anything they stated in error that contradicted the Quran or Sunnah must be discarded.[3] These scholars understood that the religion is God's religion and it is the role of humans to convey faithfully and attempt to understand— but never to distort or alter. Furthermore, they learned from the examples, as described in the Quran, of the earlier peoples who distorted their religions.

The second premise discussed earlier has to do with the historical preservation of the revelation from God. This is essential in order to verify that one is accepting the truth.

On this point, it is very difficult for the Jews to claim that they have the original Torah revealed to Moses. Unfortunately, space does not permit a detailed discussion of this topic. Hence, the conclusions of one author who discussed this topic in detail will be presented. After a lengthy discussion of the history of the Torah, Dirks concludes,

---

[1] A sect in Islam known as Shiite Islam has developed a true priesthood. This has led them to contradict this first premise.

[2] It is true that Muslims also follow the Sunnah of the Prophet in addition to the Word of God as contained in the Quran. However, this following of the Sunnah is based on direct commands in the Word of God that his Sunnah is to be followed. In fact, the place and authority of the Sunnah is affirmed in over forty places in the Quran. For more on this point, see this author's *The Authority and Importance of the Sunnah* (Denver, CO: Al-Basheer Company for Publications and Translations, 2000)

[3] Examples of such statements may be found in Zarabozo, *The Authority and Importance of the Sunnah*, pp. 82-101.

The received Torah is not a single, unitary document. It is a cut-and-paste compilation...with additional layering... While Moses, the person who received the original revelation, which the Torah is supposed to represent, lived no later than the 13th century BCE, and probably lived in the 15th century BCE, the received Torah dates to a much later epoch. The oldest identifiable substrata of the received Torah, i.e., J, can be dated no earlier than the 10th century BCE... Further, these different substrata were not combined into a received Torah until approximately 400 BCE, which would be approximately 1,000 years after the life of Moses. Still further, the received Torah was never totally standardized, with at least four different texts existing in the first century CE, which was approximately 1,500 years after the life of Moses. Additionally, if one adopts the Masoretic text as the most "official" text of the received Torah, then the oldest existing manuscript dates to circa 895 CE, which is about 2,300 years after the life of Moses. In short, although the received Torah may well contain some portions of the original Torah, the provenance of the received Torah is broken, largely unknown, and can in no way be traced to Moses.[1]

Although Jesus came many centuries after Moses, the revelation that he received did not fare much better. A group of Christians scholars known as the Fellows of the Jesus Seminar tried to determine which of the sayings attributed to Jesus can actually be

---

[1] Jerald F. Dirks, *The Cross & the Crescent* (Beltsville, MD: Amana Publications, 2001), p. 53. Other important discussions of the authenticity of the Old Testament may also be found in Maurice Bucaille, *The Bible, the Quran and Science* (Indianapolis, IN: American Trust Publications, 1978), pp. 1-43; M. M. Al-Azami, pp. 211-263.

considered authentic. They stated, "Eighty-two percent of the words ascribed to Jesus in the gospels were not actually spoken by him."[1] In describing the history of the gospels, they wrote, "The stark truth is that the history of the Greek gospels, from their creation in the first century until the discovery of the first copies of them at the beginning of the third, remains largely unknown and therefore unmapped territory."[2] Bart Ehrman's work *The Orthodox Corruption of Scripture* has identified how the scripture has been changed over time. He states his thesis, which he proves in detail, at the outset, "My thesis can be stated simply: scribes occasionally altered the words of their sacred texts to make them more patently orthodox and to prevent their misuse by Christians who espoused aberrant views."[3] That is something like putting the cart before the horse: The beliefs should be based on the transmitted texts and the texts should not be altered to fit the beliefs.

Note that these first two premises concerning the sound religion are closely related to each other. It is a general recognition on the part of many Christians that their texts have not been exactly preserved. This implies human interpolation and distortion. Since the text has been distorted in some way, it leads them to believe that they must "correct" the text. Hence, they give themselves ultimate authority to decide what the religion should be. Thus, in October 2005, the bishops of England could come up with a paper stating that there are many aspects of the Bible that one should not consider true. They go on to delineate what is true in the Bible and what is not true. If the original texts were minutely preserved, there would be no need for any correction or new authority to state what is acceptable and what is rejected.

---

[1] Robert W. Funk, Roy W. Hoover and the Jesus Seminar, *The Five Gospels: What did Jesus Really Say?* (New York: MacMillan Publishing Company, 1993), p. 5.

[2] Funk, et al., p. 9.

[3] Bart D. Ehrman, *The Orthodox Corruption of Scripture: The Effect of Early Christological Controversies on the Text of the New Testament* (New York: Oxford University Press, 1993), p. xi.

Once again, the history of Islam presents a different scenario than that of the earlier revelations. The Prophet Muhammad (peace and blessings of Allah be upon him) lived just over 1400 years ago. He is definitely the most "historical" of the various prophets.

Both the Quran and the statements of the Prophet (peace and blessings of Allah be upon him) were preserved with meticulous care. The Quran, which is not a large book, was preserved in memory as well as written form from the time of the Prophet Muhammad himself. Many of the Companions of the Prophet had memorized the entire Quran and, fearing what had happened to earlier religious communities[1], they took the necessary steps to protect it from any form of adulteration. Soon after the death of the Prophet (peace and blessings of Allah be upon him), the Quran was all compiled together and shortly afterwards official copies were sent to the distant lands to ensure that the text was pure. To this day, one can travel to any part of the world and pick up a copy Quran and find that it is the same throughout the world.[2]

Beyond the Quran, the statements of the Prophet (peace and blessings of Allah be upon him) were also preserved with great diligence. They were recorded, studied and passed on carefully from the earliest years of Islam.[3] Even the language of the Quran and the language of the Prophet has been preserved.[4] Such cannot be said for

---

[1] The Quran itself refers to the distortion of the earlier books by the previous peoples as well as their attempts to conceal some of the revelation. See, for example, Quran 5:14-15 and 4:46.

[2] A detailed history of the Quran and its preservation may be found in al-Azami, pp. 1-208. For quotes from non-Muslim writers affirming the authenticity of the Quran, see *Dialogue Between Islam and Christianity*, p. 295.

[3] There is no comprehensive work on the history of the preservation of the hadith available in English. This author is working on a book entitled, *The Preservation of the Hadith: From the Early Years*. May Allah allow it to be published soon.

[4] The differences between Classical Arabic (the language of the Quran) and Modern Standard Arabic are slight and inconsequential. One completely unfamiliar with Arabic can skim through the following book that points out when such differences occur: Elsaid Badawi, M. G. Carter and Adrian Gully, *Modern Written Arabic: A Comprehensive Grammar* (London: Routledge, 2004).

earlier prophets such as Moses and Jesus, whose Hebrew and Aramaic no longer exist.

Thus, the revelation from God as received by the Prophet Muhammad (peace and blessings of Allah be upon him) has been preserved in tact and is available to the truthseeker today.

The third parameter was related to the revelation not being superseded or abrogated. Both the Jews and the Christians understand that there was to be a Messiah after Moses who would have ultimate religious authority. The Christians say it was Jesus while the Jews say he is yet to come. The point is that if it can be shown that God is now demanding that a new message is to be followed, then, if one is truthful to God, one has no choice but to follow the new message. This point will be discussed in more detail when discussing the concept of prophethood.

The last parameter offered by this author has to do with whether the belief can be fathomed. Earlier in this work, brief refutations were made for materialists and Darwinians. Their claims are simply untenable. Similarly, the Christian belief about the Trinity is something that they themselves fought over for years and had council after council to try to determine what it truly meant. Some have simply declared it a "mystery." It does not seem that the truth as revealed by the Merciful and Wise God, who has given so many marvelous signs in the creation, should lead one to have to say as the 2nd-century North African Church Father Tertullian is well known for saying: *credo quia absurdum est*, "I believe because it is absurd." Religion should not be simply "faith-based"—a leap of faith, as such. Actually, it should be first as well "knowledge-based," so that both the heart and the mind find solace in it and submit to it with a firm resolution.

Prophethood

Jews and Christians are familiar with the concept of prophethood. Indeed, the Muslim claim is that the Prophet Muhammad (peace and blessings of Allah be upon him) is the final in a long line of prophets that included, among others, Abraham, Moses and Jesus.

The Reality of Prophethood

Messengers and prophets are specific individuals whom Allah has chosen to convey His message to humankind. He reveals to them and they in turn convey that message. The messenger must convey the message faithfully and has no right to change it or distort it any manner.[1] At the same time, after conveying, they are to be obeyed by those whom they are sent to. Allah says, "We sent no Messenger, but to be obeyed by Allah's Leave" (4:64).

Allah chooses whom He wills to be a messenger. It is not something that an individual can achieve by his own efforts. Hence, Allah says, "He sends down the angels with inspiration of His Command to whom of His servants He pleases (saying): Warn mankind that none has the right to be worshipped but I, so fear Me (by abstaining from sins and evil deeds)" (16:9). Indeed, as in the case of the Prophet Muhammad, prophethood may be something that they were originally unaware of and was not something that they were seeking. Thus, Allah says, "And thus We have sent to you (O Muhammad) an Inspiration of Our Command. You knew not what is the Book, nor what is Faith? But We have made it (this Quran) a light wherewith We guide whosoever of Our slaves We will. And verily, you (O Muhammad) are indeed guiding (mankind) to the Straight Path" (42:52). Allah also said, "And you were not expecting that the Book (this Quran) would be sent down to you, but it is a mercy from your Lord" (28:86).

This choosing of messengers is certainly not a random choice. Instead, "Allah knows best with whom to place His Message"

---

[1] See, for example, Quran 10:15 and 5:67.

(6:124). Thus, Allah chose from among humankind men of specific character.

Allah also says, "And We sent not [as Our Messengers] before you [O Muhammad] any but men, whom We inspired. So ask of those who know the Scripture if you know not" (16:43). This verse and others makes it clear that the messengers were humans. They were not semi-divine in any way whatsoever.

Allah specifically chose humans to be His messengers. The purpose of the messengers is to spread the truth from God. They make this truth clear and leave humans no excuse for not following it. Thus, the messengers are humans and not, for example, angels. If angels were sent, the purpose of simply conveying the truth and leaving the final decision to the conscience of the human to submit to that truth would have been defeated.[1] Thus, Allah says, "And they [the disbelievers] say, 'Why has not an angel been sent down to him?' Had We sent down an angel, the matter would have been judged at once, and no respite would be granted to them" (6:8).[2] In other words, everyone would have actually have no choice but to submit to and accept what the angel had brought. This was not the point. The point was to present the reality—the reality that is recognizable to the souls of mankind—in a clear and unquestionable fashion. In this way, those who are willing to accept the truth will accept it while those who do not wish to accept the truth will then reject it. This fulfills the purpose of distinguishing between those who are deserving of Allah's love and mercy and those who are deserving of Allah's wrath and punishment.

---

[1] During the time of the Prophet Muhammad, some disbelievers objected to following a mere human. Some even demanded that God should send an angel as a messenger. Hence, Allah revealed, "And nothing prevented men from believing when the guidance came to them, except that they said, 'Has Allah sent a man as (His) Messenger?' Say [to them]: 'If there were on the earth, angels walking about in peace and security, We should certainly have sent down for them from the heaven an angel as a Messenger'" (17:94-95).

[2] The verse following the above quoted words states that even if an angel would have been sent, he would have sent in the guise of a human, confusing the disbelievers even more.

Thus, the messengers came with clear guidance, glad tidings and stern warning. If Allah had not sent such messengers conveying the truth, humankind would have cried foul and claimed that they would have followed the messenger had he come to them. Allah, who knows what happened, what will happen and what possibly could happen, has said, "And if We had destroyed them with a torment before this [Messenger Muhammad], they would surely have said, 'Our Lord! If only You had sent us a Messenger, we should certainly have followed Your revelations, before we were humiliated and disgraced'" (20:134). Once the messengers are sent with the clear signs, there is no longer any excuse for humankind: "Messengers as bearers of good news as well as of warning in order that mankind should have no plea against Allah after the Messengers. And Allah is Ever All-Powerful, All-Wise" (4:165). To the astute, this verse is a grave warning indeed.[1]

As shall be discussed shortly, the sending of messengers is one of the greatest blessings that God has bestowed upon humankind.

The Sign of Prophethood

From a study of the prophets of the past, one can deduce certain "indirect" signs of prophethood. First, the individual chosen by God must have been a person of good and respected character before Allah first revealed anything to him. It would be inconceivable, for example, that someone who never lied about the matters of this world would all of a sudden begin to propagate lies about God and claim to be receiving revelation. Second, there is excellence and virtue in what he is preaching. Similarly, the basic core of his message is consistent with earlier individuals recognized to be prophets. God's basic message concerning the reality of the universe and life is not going to change from one prophet to another.

---

[1] Although the truth of monotheism is ingrained in human nature, by Allah's mercy though, He never punishes until after He sends a messenger and the message is made clear: "Whoever goes right, then he goes right only for the benefit of his ownself. And whoever goes astray, then he goes astray to his own loss. No one laden with burdens can bear another's burden. And We never punish until We have sent a Messenger (to give warning)" (17:15).

Additionally, the individual does not seek any personal benefit or payment for his conveying of the message. His goal is not a worldly one. He is conveying the message only to obey and please God. Finally, one finds that the prophet always enjoys a spiritual victory, even if he does not experience a political victory. That is, he is always content with his message, never abandons his purpose and demonstrates his resolve until his death. No one recognized as a true prophet of God has ever been known to abandon his message and beliefs.

In addition to all of that, Allah provides His messengers with special signs—something out of the ordinary to demonstrate that the individual is truly being sent by the Lord. This is all due to Allah's complete justice, mercy and goodness. He chooses and sends messengers in such a way that only the obstinate will refuse to accept the truth of the message. Hence, not only is the content of the message completely in accord with human nature, the messengers who come with the message are sent in such a way that there is again no excuse for humans not to accept them as messengers of God. As Allah says, "Indeed We have sent Our Messengers with clear proofs" (57:25).

These special signs that God bestows on the messengers are referred to as "miracles." Of course, in this age of "science," people today tend to be skeptical about the recorded miracles in the past. However, there is nothing inherently illogical about such occurrences. Starting with the premise that God has created this universe, a very defensible premise (as discussed earlier), it can also be understood that God has complete control over the workings of this universe and may alter its workings at whatever time for whomever He wills. To this day one still repeatedly hears of medical miracles or miraculous recoveries from disease—things that simply cannot be "rationally explained". No one can deny these "inexplicable" events.[1]

---

[1] Those who deny miracles will argue that somehow everything can be scientifically explained. In reality, though, at best, the scientific explanations simply describe the

In the past, there were such things as the parting of the Red Sea for Moses and the healing of the sick and blind by Jesus. These were all signs that further supported the claims of those prophets that they were being supported and guided by God. All of those, though, were signs that only those present could completely and truly appreciate. Thus, over time, people either began to doubt those stories and claims or the affects of those miracles began to wear off. However, as long as there were yet other prophets to come to revive the message, this was not a major issue.

Thus, when Allah sent His last prophet for all of humankind until the Day of Judgment, He sent him with a very different kind of miracle—still a miracle that clearly demonstrated that it has its origins with Allah but with everlasting appeal. The Prophet Muhammad (peace and blessings of Allah be upon him) said, "There was no Prophet among the Prophets but was given miracles because of which people had had belief, but what I have been given is the Divine Revelation which Allah has revealed to me. So I hope that my followers will be more than those of any other Prophet on the Day of Resurrection."[1] In other words, the Prophet Muhammad's great sign and miracle was the Quran.

Thus, the greatest sign that the Prophet Muhammad received is still being witnessed and experienced today.[2] The Quran has issued an eternal challenge for anyone to produce something similar to it. For example, Allah says, "And if you are in doubt concerning that which We have sent down [i.e., the Quran] to Our servant [Muhammad], then produce a chapter of the like thereof and call your supporters and helpers besides Allah, if you are truthful" (2:23).

The Quran is miraculous in many ways. For example, the Arabs at the time of the Prophet excelled in language. However, even

---

processes that took place. They can never touch upon the why or the how such an incident took place at that particular time or at the hand of a particular person.

[1] Recorded by al-Bukhari and Muslim.

[2] Indeed, as shall be demonstrated later, new aspects of its miraculous nature are continually being discovered.

though they greatly opposed the Prophet for many years, they realized that they could not meet the literary eloquence of the Quran.[1] But the Quran is much more than simply a "literary miracle." It is miraculous as well with respect to its fulfilled prophecies of future events, its scientific accuracy, its historical accuracy, its precise preservation, its magnanimous and wise laws, its affect that it had and still has in reforming and changing humans and so forth.

The Prophet Muhammad himself was illiterate. Still Allah chose him to be His messenger, as his illiteracy was not a deficiency in his case. It was further evidence that this illiterate Arab living just six centuries after Jesus could not have produced this book. For example, Allah revealed to the Prophet (peace and blessings of Allah be upon him) the stories of the earlier prophets. The Prophet was not living in an environment wherein he would have had much access to the teachings of the Jews or Christians. However, the stories of the prophets of old are given with precise accuracy. Actually, the case is even more astonishing. Today, many people recognize that the current Bible contains statements that are historically impossible or that are anachronisms. The Quran, though, is free of all such problematic material—another sign that it is not the product of a mere mortal.[2] In an extensive work, Fatoohi and al-Dargazelli produce many examples of Biblical errors of a historical nature not found in the Quran, although the same stories and incidents are touched upon. For example, among their many conclusions is the following,

> If the Holy Quran was derived from the Bible [as some people falsely claim, then] those many Biblical errors would have passed into it. Why, for instance, would the Holy Quran describe the

---

[1] The best discussion in English of this aspect of the miraculous nature of the Quran is Muhammad Abdullah Draz, *The Quran: An Eternal Challenge* (Leicester, United Kingdom: The Islamic Foundation, 2001), pp. 65-179.

[2] A recommended work dispelling the claims that the Quran is not a revelation from God is: Hamza Mustafa Njozi, *The Sources of the Quran: A Critical Review of the Authorship Theories* (Riyadh, Saudi Arabia: World Assembly of Muslim Youth, 1991).

Israelites as a small nation when the Bible claims that they were 2-3 million, an enormously inflated number that no scholar would accept?... Why did the Holy Quran not go along the Biblical, and indeed logical belief that Pharaoh was swallowed by the sea, to state instead that Pharaoh's "body" was rescued? And why would the Holy Quran say this about Pharaoh in particular but not about other people who were also destroyed by Allah?...[1]

Humans' Need for Messengers from God

The sending of messengers to humankind is one of Allah's greatest blessings. In describing the sending of the Prophet Muhammad, Allah says, "And We have not sent you [O Muhammad] except as a mercy for all that exists" (12:107).

Humans are actually in great need of this blessing from Allah. They are in need of a practical example to show how one should lead one's life to please Allah. They are desperately also in need of the knowledge that these messengers brought.

Had Allah willed, Allah could have simply revealed His message in written form on mountainsides, for example. However, there is a great blessing and wisdom in His sending of human messengers instead. The benefit of these messengers are twofold: (1) By sending human messengers instead of simply communicated or written word, Allah has transformed His message from the realm of the abstract to the realm of the practical. The implementation of the message by the messenger gives humans a practical implementation of the guidance. The guidance is not simply vague, general principles that anyone could understand in a variety of ways. No, the message has been given in a concrete and practical format with detailed

---

[1] Louay Fatoohi and Shetha al-Dargazelli, *History Testifies to the Infallibility of the Quran: Early History of the Children of Israel* (Delhi, India: Adam Publishers & Distributors, 1999), pp. 247-248.

examples for humans to follow.[1] (2) Although messengers were humans of excellent character, they were still mere humans. In fact, they were humans who were meant to be examples for others. Hence, by their implementation of the divine teachings, it demonstrates that these teachings are practicable and within the means of humans. No one should think of righteousness as something beyond human capacity. It is within human capacity and the actions of the prophets are a proof of that.

As noted above, humans are also in desperate need for the knowledge that the messengers convey. This knowledge can be divided into two types, both being essential to humans.[2]

The first type of knowledge is that of the supernatural, or what the Islamic texts call the "unseen." Again, these are matters beyond the realm of human experience. Humans can know about these issues only via revelation from Allah. This realm includes detailed knowledge about Allah and His attributes, the purpose of creation, how can one distinguish between good and evil, what occurs to humankind after death and in the hereafter and so forth. This knowledge lies at the core of the religion and humankind cannot live properly without basing life on these articles of faith.

However, Allah's guidance is not concerned only with those issues. Allah's guidance that He revealed to His human messengers

---

[1] One important difference between Judaism, Christianity and Islam is that the detailed examples of the lives of the prophets have been lost in the case of Judaism and Christianity. Under many circumstances—even the very process of prayer itself—Jews and Christians do not have a definite example to turn to. Hence, they end up in doubt, confused, divided and separated. Muslims, on the other hand, can all rally around the detailed example of the Prophet Muhammad that has been preserved for posterity. Hence, for example, one can enter mosques throughout the world today and find Muslims praying in the same fashion— all based on the divine guidance as enacted by the Prophet Muhammad (peace and blessings of Allah be upon him).

[2] In reality, both types of knowledge are related to one issue: the proper way of worshipping and submitting to Allah. In Islam, ritual acts of worship as well as "mundane" activities all fall under the realm of religion and all must be done in accordance with Allah's revelation. The two types are being distinguished above in order to emphasize that "worldly matters" definitely also need to be subjected to Allah's guidance.

also guides humans in worldly or mundane affairs. Except for technological matters that Allah has easily put within the reach of humans, humans are just as much in need of Allah's guidance on these issues. It is Allah, the Creator, the Fashioner, alone who knows what is best for humans. Allah has said, "Should not He Who has created know? And He is the Most Kind and Courteous (to His servants), All-Aware (of everything)" (67:14). This point needs further elaboration because it strikes at the root of secularism, which is dominating the world's thinking today.

Humans have attempted to construct their own economic systems, political systems, international laws and so on. When doing so, though, they have to admit that they are attempting something that is beyond their means. Thus, the harms of what they produce many times outweigh the good, even with the best of intentions.

In the realm of economics, the first thing that may come to mind is the collapse of the theories of socialism and communism. One should, though, also take a closer look at capitalism and how far its reality is from what it is supposed to be. The early capitalist theorists envisioned a theory that would lead to "the best of all possible worlds." However, their theories were based on assumptions that never were and never will be fulfilled. They assumed perfect competition, perfect knowledge, free trade and so forth. Once these assumptions are violated, which they inevitably are, they do not lead to the "best of all possible worlds." Instead, they have led to a world of exploitation, wherein the rich get richer and the poor get poorer. Even though governments have recognized the ultimate failures and have tried to step in to remedy the situation, as long as the "free market" is the driving force, profit is the ultimate goal and demand drives what is being produced, the world will remain far from the "best of all possible worlds."[1] It is dumbfounding to think that untold

---

[1] A classic example of human reasoning relates to a concept developed in the Western world known as "natural law," law that is supposedly just, inherent and recognizable by all throughout the world. In particular, as Westerners relied less on scripture, they turned more and more to concepts such as natural law and other branches of secularism. As Spain was

numbers of children are dying daily in lesser-developed countries due to the "tool" of modern capitalism: interest. Some African governments are forced to spend more on debt servicing than they spend on health or education.[1] Of course, this deadly interest is and will forever be forbidden in Islam.

In general, man-made laws, as opposed to revelation from God, are susceptible to four distinct problems. First, humans are repeatedly influenced by desires. In the Quran, truth is often juxtaposed with the following of one's desires. One can either follow what is true and correct—which is known through revelation—or follow desires, including what humans claim to be "good." In one verse, for example, Allah says, "Judge between them by what Allah has revealed, and follow not their vain desires, diverging away from the truth that has come to you" (5:48). Thus, one can find an emphasis on "freedoms" and "rights" in man-made laws rather than an overall consideration of what is best for society or the world as a whole. Perhaps alcohol and sexual freedom are two good examples of this nature. How much harm and cost is incurred by society due to the

---

moving across the new world, Francesco Victoria was asked whether the Christians could use military force to convert the Indians to Christianity. His reply was in the negative. However, he further stated that the Spaniards, by natural law, had the "right" to preach Christianity as well as the right to pass through Indian lands. If the Indians refused these two, which they should know by virtue of the fact that it is natural law, the Spaniards would then have the right to use military force against them. As James Turner Johnson wrote, "The rights of which Victoria spoke were conceived by him as universal, as 'natural'; yet the Indians knew nothing of them. They were in fact historically derived from the customary practices of European societies. In the name of natural law Victoria was justifying cultural imperialism." James Turner Johnson, "Historical Roots and Sources of the Just War Tradition in Western Culture," in John Kelsay and James Turner Johnson, *Historical and Theoretical Perspectives On War And Peace In Western And Islamic Traditions* (New York: Greenwood Press, 1991), p. 26. Also see p. 17 of the same work. Bainton also notes Victoria's reasoning and then states, "Later the great theologian Sepulveda adapted the theory of the just war to the new situation by having recourse to its most ancient formulation declared by Aristotle, who had said that a just war is one waged to enslave those who by nature are destined to be slaves and who resist their destiny." Roland H. Bainton, *Christian Attitudes Toward War & Peace: A Historical Survey and Critical Re-Evaluation* (Nashville, TN: Abingdon Press, 1990), p. 166.

[1] Cf., Noreena Hertz. *The Debt Threat* (New York: HarperBusiness, 2004), p. 3.

legality of alcohol? How many homes are torn apart due to alcohol, how many women are beaten due to alcohol and how many people cannot function in society due to alcohol? Yet one dare not question the "right"—actually the desire—to drink. The same is true with sexual freedoms. AIDS, which is first and foremost transmitted by sexual contact, for example, is causing great harm in the world in terms of lives and economic costs. Actually, the Prophet Muhammad (peace and blessings of Allah be upon him) foretold such when he said, "Illicit sexual intercourse does not spread among a people to the extent that it becomes public except that epidemics and ailments will spread among them that the people had never experienced before."[1]

Even if humans are able to raise themselves above any passions and desires on their part, they have to realize that there is a great deal of difference between the natural sciences and social sciences. Social scientists realize that they are on a slippery slope. They have no labs or vacuums in which they can test theories. The interaction between various components of human life is simply too great for any human or group of humans to study completely. Even if they are not biased, too many factors, such as environment, may distort their views. Some even doubt if any real truths can be determined by such sciences.[2] In the Quran, Allah speaks about such limited ability on the part of humankind: "They know only the outside appearance of the life of the world" (30:7). If such is admitted, it demonstrates that humans are in need of guidance and

---

[1] Recorded by ibn Maajah and al-Haakim. Authenticated by al-Albaani. See al-Albaani, *Saheeh al-Jaami*, vol. 2, p. 1321.

[2] A good summary of the different difficulties they face is found in the following passage: "They [the various social sciences] work with different methods, different forms of knowledge, and different criteria by which that knowledge is judged. More important, the social world itself is complex, involving a number of different objects which do not fall easily into the province of any one social science – economics, history, sociology, social psychology and psychology all study interactions between human beings, from different perspectives and with different ends in view. Human beings are all also objects of biology and other natural sciences which produce their own knowledge of the social world." Ted Benton and Ian Craib, *Philosophy of Social Science: The Philosophical Foundations of Social Thought* (New York: Palgrave, 2001), p. 174.

knowledge from their Creator, who had graciously sent such guidance through his prophets.[1] In fact, according to the scholars of Islamic Law, the attaining and fulfilling of the main needs and necessities of human life is the basic purpose and goal of the law propagated by the prophets.

Finally, secular laws cannot inspire humans like divine revelation can. There can be no effective moral influence in such laws.[2] In other words, except for the use of force, there is nothing in man-made laws to drive a person to comply with such laws. However, adherence to the laws promulgated by the prophets is driven by a desire to please God and to avoid His wrath. When this feeling penetrates the heart, nothing can keep the individual from following God's laws—no temptations, bribes, money and so forth.

None of the above critiques that this author has made are startling or new. One could argue that they are all obvious and logical. The question then is: Why doesn't humankind turn to God's guidance and the teachings of the messengers since it is logically what is best for humankind? The dominant paradigm today is that which is built upon Western civilization. Western civilization, due to its own historical circumstances, deemed it wise to discard revelation in "public" matters. One could perhaps argue that such was understandable given that the West did not have access to a preserved revelation from God. However, once people realize that God's revelation is available and exactly preserved in the Quran, it is hoped that more and more of them will turn to it and guide their lives by it.

---

[1] Of course, another problem that one sees in many societies today is that of "power." In general, wealth breeds power. Power, in turn, allows one to influence legislation, many times against the interests of society.

[2] It is interesting to see how this role is sometimes relegated to religion in otherwise non-religious societies. In essence, the individual is told not to believe in any of the laws of the religion but one should believe in the fact that one should act morally. However, if the laws of the religion are false or not worth applying, why should the moral recommendations of the religion be considered worthy applying?

In sum, there is no escaping the fact that humans are gravely in need of the knowledge vouchsafed via the prophets and they are also in need of the example that the prophets established.

The Principles of the Messengers' Call

It has been narrated that the Prophet (peace and blessings of Allah be upon him) said that Allah had sent 124,000 prophets.[1] Allah stated that He sent a messenger to every nation (Quran 16:36). Some of them are spoken about in the Quran while others are not mentioned.[2]

Even though so many prophets and messengers were sent, they were actually all along the same path. As the prophet described them, they are all one big family of brethren. The Prophet said, "We, prophets, are brothers descending from the same father and several mothers, and sharing the same religion."[3]

Indeed, Allah tells the Prophet (peace and blessings of Allah be upon him) that He is guiding the Prophet to the same religion as his predecessors. Allah says, "He (Allah) has ordained for you the same religion which He ordained for Noah, and that which We have inspired in you (O Muhammad), and that which We ordained for Abraham, Moses and Jesus..." (42:13). In another verse, referring to the prophets as a whole, Allah says, "Truly! This, your religion is one religion, and I am your Lord, therefore worship Me (Alone)" (21:92).

---

[1] Recorded by Ahmad. The narration also states that among them, 315 were also messengers. Messengers are slightly different from prophets. The difference is of no concern here.

[2] Allah says, "And, indeed We have sent Messengers before you (O Muhammad); of some of them We have related to you their story and of some We have not related to you their story" (40:78).

[3] Recorded by al-Bukhari and Muslim.

Thus, a Muslim believes in all of those different prophets and messengers and, with respect to belief in them and honoring them, does not differentiate between any among them. God sent all of them. They were all believing in the same essential truths and calling to similar paths. Hence, one has no right to say that he will believe and respect some of them and reject, belie or disrespect others. In the first place, this would be disrespectful to God, who sent each and every one of them. It would also be illogical since they all came with essentially the same message and were, as the Prophet described, brothers to one another.

Hence, they all must be believed in and given the proper respect. Thus, Allah says, "Say (O Muslims), 'We believe in Allah and that which has been sent down to us and that which has been sent down to Abraham, Ishmael, Isaac, Jacob, and to the twelve sons of Jacob, and that which has been given to Moses and Jesus, and that which has been given to the Prophets from their Lord. We make no distinction between any of them, and to Him we have submitted (in Islam)'" (2:136; also see 3:84). In sum, since they were all sent by the one and only God and since the truth of this existence is one and not changing, it is the case that their messages were essential one and the same.

Studying the Quran, one can see the basic principles of all of the messengers' call. Their message revolved around the following three points:

(1) Calling people to God, explaining with clear proofs that there is none worthy of worship except Him and inviting them to submit to Him alone and to renounce any and all false gods: This is the essence of the true religion and it has been so since the time of Adam. All the different nations and peoples of the earth were given this message. Allah says, "And verily, We have sent among every nation a Messenger (proclaiming): 'Worship Allah (Alone), and avoid all false deities'" (16:36). Allah also says, "And We did not send any Messenger before you (O Muhammad) but We inspired him (saying), 'None has the right to be worshipped but I (Allah), so

worship Me (Alone and none else)'" (21:25). In the Quran, Allah quotes the following words from many different messengers: "O my people, worship Allah (alone) for you have no other god beside Him" (7:59, 65, 73, 85 and elsewhere).

(2) Showing that there is a specific path of conduct leading to God's pleasure and the purifying of one's soul that each individual is obliged to adhere to: In addition to the correct belief about God, there is also the issue of correct acts of worship and practice of said belief. Hence, the messengers did not simply tell people to worship God. They also received revelation concerning how God is to be worshipped and what is the way of life one is supposed to follow in this worldly existence. The path includes ritual acts of worship as well as worldly laws and moral guidance. Every people were guided to such a straight path. Allah says, "To each among you, We have prescribed a law and a clear way" (5:48). However, all of the prophets brought the same basic path containing the same general laws, such as commandment to pray, prohibition of polytheism, prohibition of adultery, prohibition of murder and so forth. This does not mean that there were no differences whatsoever concerning their particular practices. In general, their practices were similar but God sent many prophets to specific peoples with specific laws for their time and place. This is part of Allah's mercy and wisdom. This variation in some of their practices does not imply any contradiction concerning their basic message or even the basic nature of their paths. In fact, even for one prophet, some of his specific practices may change over time. For example, the Prophet Muhammad and his followers used to face Jerusalem while praying. This practice was abrogated by the revelation instructing the Muslims to face Mecca. The Prophet and his followers were still along the same path of submission to Allah, but this particular law had changed as Allah had so decreed.

(3) Explaining the fates of individuals when they decide to accept and worship Allah and when they decide to refuse to submit to or worship Allah: On this point, the messengers taught humankind about life after death, resurrection, final judgment and reward or

punishment from Allah. The details of these matters can only be known from Allah and Allah never punished any people until the messenger had made these points clear to them. Thus, all the messengers actually came with glad tidings for those who wish to accept faith and stern warnings of a ominous end for those who wish to reject it. Allah says, "And We send not the Messengers but as givers of glad tidings and as warners. So whosoever believes and does righteous good deeds, upon such shall come no fear, nor shall they grieve. But those who reject Our proofs, the torment will touch them for their disbelief" (6:48-49).

The above are the three basic points around which all the messages revolved. They are the keys to proper living in both this life and the Hereafter. The stories of the prophets in the Quran demonstrate that these were the main issues of concern. The prophets strove to convey their messages, fulfilled their trusts and conveyed the messages clearly. Once the above points are proclaimed, there is no longer any room left for debate or excuse. The prophet has fulfilled his mission and now the matter is left to the individual.

The Foretelling of the Prophet Muhammad in Earlier Scriptures

The previous section showed that the basic message of all of the prophets were the same. In addition, it was definitely the role of some, if not all, of the earlier prophets to foretell the coming of the Prophet Muhammad. Allah says in the Quran, "Those who follow the Messenger, the Prophet who can neither read nor write (i.e., Muhammad) whom they find written with them in the Torah and the Gospel..." (7:157). Allah also says, "And (remember) when Jesus, son of Mary, said, 'O Children of Israel! I am the Messenger of Allah unto you confirming the [Torah which came] before me, and giving glad tidings of a Messenger to come after me, whose name shall be Ahmad.[1] But when he came to them with clear proofs, they said, 'This is plain magic'" (61:6).

---

[1] Ahmad is another name for the Prophet Muhammad (peace and blessings of Allah be upon him) and comes from the same root.

Based on these and other verses of the Quran, Muslim scholars realized that there must exist some evidence of the coming of the Prophet (peace and blessings of Allah be upon him) in what is left of the original scriptures of the Jews and Christians. Indeed, many verses have been found that seem to point directly to the Prophet Muhammad. (Actually, a number of books have been written on this topic.[1]) However, as is often the case with Biblical interpretation, the understanding of a particular verse may not be clear and others may read the same verse that the Muslims point to in a very different manner. Having said that, though, there still remain some verses for which the only plausible interpretation seems to be the Prophet Muhammad (peace and blessings of Allah be upon him).

For the sake of brevity, only a couple of examples will be discussed. The first of these passages comes from the Old Testament. Moses is speaking and says,

> And the LORD said unto me, They have well spoken that which they have spoken. I will raise them up a Prophet from among their brethren, like unto thee, and will put my words in his mouth; and he shall speak unto them all that I shall command him. And it shall come to pass, that whosoever will not hearken unto my words which he shall speak in my name, I will require it of him (Deuteronomy 18:17-19, *King James Version*).

Perhaps the first question that needs to be answered is who are the brethren of the Israelites. According to the *Hebrew Dictionary of the Bible*, the term brethren refers to a "personification of a group of tribes who were regarded as near kinsmen of Israelites."[2] A group that fits that description very well were the descendants of Ishmael,

---

[1] One of the most scholarly and detailed is *Muhammad in the Bible* by Abdul-Ahad Dawud. Dawud was a former priest and has an in-depth analysis of the language of many Biblical verses.

[2] Quoted in Jamal Badawi, *Muhammad in the Bible* (Halifax, Canada: Islamic Information Foundation, n.d.), p. 40.

the son of Abraham and the half-brother of Isaac. It is from Ishmael that the Arabs, and Muhammad in particular, are descended.

Secondly, the coming prophet is described as being "like unto thee," that is, similar to Moses. Now there are Christians who claim that this passage is a reference to Jesus. Given that Christians do not consider Jesus simply a prophet, this is highly unlikely. Nevertheless, Jamal Badawi has constructed a table that demonstrates how similar Moses and Muhammad were (and how dissimilar Jesus was to them). Here is the bulk of Badawi's table:[1]

Area of Comparison	Moses	Muhammad	Jesus
Birth	Usual	Usual	Unusual
Family life	Married, children	Married, children	No marriage or children
Death	Usual	Usual	Unusual
Career	Prophet/Statesmen	Prophet/Statesmen	Prophet
Forced Emigration	To Median	To Madinah	None
Encounter with enemies	Hot pursuit	Hot pursuit, battles	No similar encounter
Results of encounter	Moral/Physical victory	Moral/Physical victory	Moral victory
Nature of teachings	Spiritual/legal	Spiritual/legal	Spiritual
Acceptance of leadership by his people	Rejected then accepted	Rejected then accepted	Rejected (by most Israelites)

---

[1] Badawi, p. 41.

The verses above then continue by saying, "and will put my words in his mouth; and he shall speak unto them all that I shall command him." This is an absolutely accurate description of the Prophet Muhammad in relation to the Quran. The words were put into his mouth via direct revelation from Gabriel, wherein Muhammad repeated verbatim what was revealed to him and he commanded all that the revelation contained.

In the New Testament[1], one can find the following passages in the *Gospel of John*, "If ye love me, keep my commandments. And I will pray the Father, and he shall give you another Comforter, that he may abide with you for ever" (John 14:15-16). Elsewhere it states, "Nevertheless I tell you the truth; It is expedient for you that I go away: for if I go not away, the Comforter will not come unto you; but if I depart, I will send him unto you. And when he is come, he will reprove the world of sin, and of righteousness, and of judgment" (John 16:7-8). It also states, "I have yet many things to say unto you, but ye cannot bear them now. Howbeit when he, the Spirit of truth, is come, he will guide you into all truth: for he shall not speak of himself; but whatsoever he shall hear, that shall he speak: and he will show you things to come" (John 16:12-13).

Who is this who is to come after Christ and that cannot come while Christ is present? The Christians interpret these passages as referring to the Holy Ghost. But Christian theology states that the Father, the Son and the Holy Ghost are all part of the trinity, together as one being. If this is the case, how is the one present and the other is not present? Such is completely incompatible with Christian

---

[1] For more on prophecies in the New Testament, see Misha'al ibn Abdullah, *What Did Jesus REALLY Say?* (Ann Arbor, MI: Islamic Assembly of North America, 2001), pp. 358-463. In *The Oxford Companion to the Bible*, it states, "Jesus certainly thought of himself as a prophet (Mark 6:4; Luke 13.33) but there was a final quality about his message and work that entitles us to conclude that he thought of himself as God's final, definitive emissary to Israel." (Quoted in Al-Azami, p. 273.) This was certainly true—he was the final prophet of the tribes of Israel. However, as the passages above disclose, it is clear that Jesus also knew that he was not the last of all the prophets.

theology. Furthermore, the portion in the last segment quoted, "he will guide you into all truth: for he shall not speak of himself; but whatsoever he shall hear, that shall he speak: and he will show you things to come," is nothing but another beautiful description of the Prophet (peace and blessings of Allah be upon him) and how he received and passed on the revelation from God.

One last set of verses will be presented that this author believes require virtually no comment other than saying that a great prophet was still expected: "And this is the record of John, when the Jews sent priests and Levites from Jerusalem to ask him, Who art thou? And he confessed, and denied not; but confessed, I am not the Christ. And they asked him, What then? Art thou Elias?[1] And he saith, I am not. Art thou that prophet? And he answered, No" (John 1:19-21, *King James Version*). Who was that Prophet that John and the Jews were expecting?

These brief examples will have to suffice and the interested reader may consult more in-depth works. However, if these signs do point to the Prophet Muhammad (peace and blessings of Allah be upon him) as Muslim scholars maintain, then, in sincerity to the Prophet who originally made the statement, one has to follow the prophet he pointed to.

The Final Message

Allah had sent numerous prophets throughout the centuries. However, He had determined that He should send a final messenger with a final message. This final messenger would be the messenger for all of humankind from his time until the Day of Reckoning. There was to be no later revelation and no later prophet to bring any changes to this revelation. Hence, this one had to differ from the previous in some ways.

First, since no one could come later to correct any mistakes or distortions, the revelation received by the last prophet had to be preserved in its pristine purity.

---

[1] In Matthew 17:12 Jesus is recorded as stating that Elias had already come.

Second, the nature of the "sign" of the last prophet would have to be different as well. This is because this sign would have to affect not only the people who were alive during the time of the prophet but also all those who would come later.

Third, this final prophet could not simply be sent for one community among humankind—each then having their own final prophet and then differing with one another. This final prophet had to be sent for all of humankind, putting an end to the succession of prophets and being suitable for the world as a whole.

Fourth, the laws and teachings of this message had to be fixed in matters that need to be fixed for all of humankind until the Day of Judgment and guiding yet flexible or accommodating in those matters that need to be open to change due to the changing circumstances of humankind.

On all of these points, one sees that it is the message of the Prophet Muhammad (peace and blessings of Allah be upon him) that fits all of these criteria. The exacting preservation of the Quran and the Sunnah was already discussed. Similarly, the nature of his "sign," the Quran, the ultimate miracle that can still be experienced today, was also discussed earlier.

As for the third issue, the Prophet Muhammad (peace and blessings of Allah be upon him) was the only prophet to make it known that he was not sent only for a certain people but he was sent for all the various peoples of the world. The Jews, for example, consider themselves to be a chosen race and that their message is meant exclusively for themselves. Thus, many orthodox Jews do not believe in proselytizing their faith. The New Testament also makes it clear that Jesus' mission was to the Tribes of Israel. Matthew 10: 5-6 read: "These twelve Jesus sent forth, and commanded them, saying, Go not into the way of the Gentiles, and into any city of the Samaritans enter ye not: But go rather to the lost sheep of the house of Israel." Jesus is reported to have said when the Canaanite woman came to him for help, "I am not sent but unto the lost sheep of the house of Israel" (Matthew 15:24).[1] This limited mission of Jesus' is also affirmed in the Quran (61:6).

In the case of the Prophet Muhammad (peace and blessings of Allah be upon him), however, Allah says, "Say (O Muhammad to the people), 'O mankind! Verily, I am sent to you all as the Messenger of Allah' (7:158). Another verse reads, "And We have not sent you (O Muhammad) except as a giver of glad tidings and a warner to all mankind" (34:28). There are yet other verses giving the same purport. The Prophet Muhammad also stated that he was distinguished from the earlier prophets by five matters. The last he mentioned was, "The prophet would be sent to his people only while I have been sent to all of mankind."[2]

Finally, when one studies the law promulgated by the Prophet Muhammad (peace and blessings of Allah be upon him) one finds that it has the needed elements of flexibility that allow it to be just as practicable today as it was during the time of the Prophet.[3] What needs to be fixed forever is fixed in Islamic law. What needs to be left flexible is left flexible. For example, in business dealings, interest is prohibited forever. In addition to that, general guidelines are given. However, the guidance is such that when new forms of business dealings are developed, as in modern times, one can determine which are acceptable according to Islamic guidelines and which are not. Thus, Islamic Law has been proven to be feasible for over 1400 years and, according to Islamic beliefs, will continue to be feasible until the Day of Judgment.

---

[1] In the same context, Jesus in quoted in Matthew 15:26 as saying about helping the Canaanite woman, "It is not meet to take the children's bread, and cast it to dogs." Again, God alone knows what parts of the Gospels attributed to Jesus were actually said by him.

[2] Recorded by al-Bukhari and Muslim.

[3] One of the descriptions of the Prophet given in the Quran is, "he commands them for what is good; and forbids them from evil; he allows them as lawful all good things, and prohibits them as unlawful all foul things; and he releases them from their heavy burdens, and from the fetters (bindings) that were upon them" (7:157).

The Seal of the Prophets

After so many prophets sent by Allah, Allah sent the Prophet Muhammad. Muhammad was born around 570 years after the birth of Jesus Christ. He was born in Mecca, in the Arabian Peninsula. The people of Mecca were devoted to idol-worship. In Mecca, there was a building built by the prophets Abraham and Ishmael. This structure, known as the Kabah, was dedicated to the worship of Allah, the only true God. The Arab polytheists, though, filled it with their idols. Muhammad lived among them but never took part in idol-worship. He was known for his honesty and had the nickname, "the trustworthy."

At the age of forty, Muhammad received his first revelation. Although this was at first startling to him, he then understood the mission he had from God. The polytheistic Arabs quickly rejected his message, that none is to be worshipped except God. Although he was known as "the trustworthy," they belied him and soon after started a massive campaign to persecute those who believed in Muhammad. Some of his followers were forced to flee to Abyssinia. After thirteen years of preaching in Mecca, the Prophet himself was forced to leave to the city of Madinah, where he already had some followers. They made him the leader of the city. The disbelievers of Mecca did not rest and attempted to militarily squash the new faith. However, what was originally a small band of Muslims grew in number and were able to withstand the onslaught of the disbelievers. Within ten years, the Prophet himself led an army back to Mecca and conquered it in a bloodless victory. Thus, Islam became victorious in Arabia and began spreading throughout the world.[1]

Allah decreed that this Prophet Muhammad (peace and blessings of Allah be upon him) should be His final messenger. Allah says, "Muhammad is not the father of any man among you, but he is

---

[1] An interesting work refuting the possibility of Muhammad (peace and blessings of Allah be upon him) being a false prophet is Abdul Radhi Muhammad Abdul Mohsen, *Muhammad's Prophethood: Reality or Hoax* (Riyadh, Saudi Arabia: International Islamic Publishing House, 1999).

the Messenger of Allah and the seal of the Prophets. And Allah is Ever All-Aware of everything" (33:40). The Prophet Muhammad (peace and blessings of Allah be upon him) himself said, "I have been sent to all of the creation and the prophets have been sealed by me."[1] Again, he said, "The Children of Israel were led by the prophets; whenever a prophet died, a prophet succeeded (him). Lo! There will be no prophet after me"[2]

Thus, there finally came the Prophet who explicitly declared that he is the final prophet. No prophet shall come after him. The truth of his message and his own honesty are well established. If one comes to the conclusion that he is to be believed or that the Quran is true, then it is also to be believed on this point as well.

Hence, no one has the right to accept the other prophets while rejecting the Prophet Muhammad. No one has the right to say that Muhammad was truthful but, "I chose to still follow Jesus or Moses instead." Logically speaking, one should not expect this to be acceptable to Allah. Allah has sent His final messenger to be believed in and followed, superseding and canceling what is left of the teachings of earlier prophets. In the Quran, Allah describes such an attitude: "And when it is said to them, 'Believe in what Allah has sent down,' they say, 'We believe in what was sent down to us.' And they disbelieve in that which came after it, while it is the truth confirming what is with them" (2:91). Allah has further declared people of this nature to be disbelievers. He has said, "Verily, those who disbelieve in Allah and His Messengers and wish to make distinction between Allah and His Messengers (by believing in Allah and disbelieving in His Messengers) saying, 'We believe in some but reject others,' and wish to adopt a way in between. They are in truth disbelievers. And We have prepared for the disbelievers a humiliating torment. And those who believe in Allah and His Messengers and make no distinction between any of them, We shall give them their

---

[1] Recorded by Muslim.
[2] Recorded by al-Bukhari and Muslim.

rewards, and Allah is Ever Oft-Forgiving, Most Merciful" (4:150-152).

The Prophet said, "[I swear] by [God], the One in whose hand is my soul, there will be none of my addressed people, be he Jew or Christian, who hears of me and dies without believing in that with which I was sent except that he will be from the inhabitants of the Hell-fire."[1] The Prophet even told one of his companions, "If my brother Moses were alive today, he would have no option but to follow me."[2]

In sum, the signs pointing to the Prophet beforehand are there. The Prophet's own honesty are unquestionable. The preservation of his scripture is established. All the indicators point to his prophethood. As a prophet, his word must be believed in. He has declared himself the last prophet and said that all of humankind must now choose to follow him. This is the choice facing every one of humankind and it is hoped that they will make the correct and logical decision.

---

[1] Recorded by Muslim.
[2] Recorded by Ahmad and al-Daarimi.

Islam
The Definition of Islam

Lexically, the word *islam* is the verbal noun of the verb which means, "He resigned, or submitted, himself."[1] Hence, *islam* is the way or act of submitting and resigning oneself. "Muslim" is the active participle of the verb meaning "to submit." Hence, a "muslim" is one who submits.

One will note from the above that the word Islam does not mean "peace," although one can hear that stated quite often recently. It is true that the word Islam and the Arabic word for peace (*salaam*) both come from the same root. Indeed, there is a close connection between the two. Islam is the source of true peace. Of course, what is meant here is not simply peace as in "an absence of a state of war." Peace means much more than that. One can be free of war yet still suffer from anxiety or despair and lack peace. Here, it is referring to a complete sense of peace. Islam brings about a complete tranquility and peace of mind that is the result of realizing that one is believing and acting in accord with the guidance of one's Creator. This internal peace can then spread to the family, the community, the society and the world as a whole.[2] It is a special form of tranquility that can only be produced by the proper belief in God. Hence, Allah says, "[This Quran] wherewith Allah guides all those who seek His Good Pleasure to ways of peace, and He brings them out of darkness by His Will unto light and guides them to a Straight Way" (5:16). For those who follow this path, their ultimate reward will be the abode of peace: "For them will be the home of peace (Paradise) with their Lord" (6:127). In sum, it is not correct to say, "Islam means peace," but certainly true peace comes only via Islam.

As a technical term, the word Islam has three distinguishable usages: (1) It is a term used for the true religion of

---

[1] E. W. Lane, *Arabic-English Lexicon* (Cambridge, England: The Islamic Texts Society, 1984), vol.1, p. 1413.

[2] On this point, one can read Sayyed Qutb, *Islam and Universal Peace* (Indianapolis, IN: American Trust Publications, 1977), *passim.*

God since the time of the creation of humans; (2) It is a term used today for the religion brought by the last prophet, Prophet Muhammad; and (3) It refers to the outward act of submitting to Allah as opposed to the inward acts of faith. The first two definitions shall be discussed in more detail here and the last in a later section.

Islam: The Religion of All of the Prophets

As stated above, lexically, *islam* means submitting and resigning oneself. In a religious sense, the term is used to mean, "the true submission and obedience to God alone." Thus, Nomani states,

> Literally, Islam denotes self-surrender or to give oneself up to someone and accept his overlordship in the fullest sense of the term. The religion sent down by God and brought into the world by His Apostles has been called Islam for the simple reason that, in it, the bondsman yields completely to the power and control of the Lord and makes the rendering of whole-hearted obedience to Him the cardinal principle of his life. This is the sum and substance of the Islamic creed...[1]

In this sense, then, it was the religion of all of the true prophets of God. In fact, it was the religion of all of their followers as well. In other words, every true believer from the time of Adam to the last believer on earth practices Islam and is a Muslim. Furthermore, it is the only religion that Allah ever commanded humankind to follow. Islam, therefore, is the only religion that has ever been acceptable to Allah. Allah says, "Truly, the religion with Allah is Islam (submission to Him)" (3:19). Allah also says, "And whoever seeks a religion other than Islam, it will never be accepted of him, and in the Hereafter he will be one of the losers" (3:85).

Throughout the Quran, Allah makes it clear that the religion and practice of all the prophets was that of Islam. For example, Allah quotes Noah as saying, after explaining the faith to the people, "But if

---

[1] Mohammad Manzoor Nomani, *Meaning and Message of the Traditions* (Lucknow, India: Academy of Islamic Research and Publications, 1975), vol. 1, p. 54.

you turn away [from accepting my doctrine to worship none but Allah], then no reward have I asked of you, my reward is only from Allah, and I have been commanded to be one of the Muslims" (10:71).

The following passage concerns Abraham and is quite instructive, deserving to be quoted at length:

> And (remember) when Abraham and (his son) Ishmael were raising the foundations of the House [in Mecca], (saying), "Our Lord! Accept (this service) from us. Verily! You are the All-Hearer, the All-Knower. Our Lord! And make us submissive [Muslims] unto You and of our offspring a nation submissive [Muslims] unto You, and show us our ceremonies of pilgrimage, and accept our repentance. Truly, You are the One Who accepts repentance, the Most Merciful. Our Lord! Send amongst them[1] a Messenger of their own, who shall recite unto them Your Verses and instruct them in the Book and Wisdom, and purify them. Verily! You are the All-Mighty, the All-Wise."
>
> And who turns away from the religion of Abraham except him who befools himself? Truly, We chose him in this world and verily, in the Hereafter he will be among the righteous. When his Lord said to him, "Submit (i.e. be a Muslim)!" He said, "I have submitted myself (as a Muslim) to the Lord of the worlds." And this (submission to Allah, Islam) was enjoined by Abraham upon his sons and by Jacob, (saying), "O my sons! Allah has chosen for you the (true) religion, then die not except as Muslims." Or were you witnesses when death approached Jacob? When he said unto his sons, "What will you

---

[1] The descendants of Ishmael. Ishmael was the son of Abraham and Muhammad was a descendant of Ishmael.

worship after me?" They said, "We shall worship your God, the God of your fathers, Abraham, Ishmael, Isaac, One God, and to Him we submit (in Islam)."

That was a nation who has passed away. They shall receive the reward of what they earned and you of what you earn. And you will not be asked of what they used to do. And they say, "Be Jews or Christians, then you will be guided." Say (to them, O Muhammad), "Nay, (we follow) only the religion of Abraham, of pure monotheism, and he was not of those who worshipped others along with Allah." Proclaim (O Muslims), "We believe in Allah and that which has been sent down to us and that which has been sent down to Abraham, Ishmael, Isaac, Jacob, and to the twelve sons of Jacob, and that which has been given to Moses and Jesus, and that which has been given to the Prophets from their Lord. We make no distinction between any of them, and to Him we have submitted (in Islam)." So if they believe in the like of that which you believe, then they are rightly guided, but if they turn away, then they are only in opposition. So Allah will suffice you against them. And He is the All- Hearer, the All-Knower. [Our religion is] the Religion of Allah and which religion can be better than Allah's? And we are His worshippers.

Say [O Muhammad to the Jews and Christians], "Dispute you with us about Allah while He is our Lord and your Lord? And we are to be rewarded for our deeds and you for your deeds. And we are sincere to Him in worship and obedience."

Or do you say that Abraham, Ishmael, Isaac, Jacob and the twelve sons of Jacob were Jews or

Christians? Say, "Do you know better or does Allah [know better that they all were Muslims]? And who is more unjust than he who conceals the testimony he has from Allah? And Allah is not unaware of what you do." That was a nation who has passed away. They shall receive the reward of what they earned, and you of what you earn. And you will not be asked of what they used to do. (2:127-141).

A number of illuminating points come from this passage. First, though, it should be noted that Abraham is often called in the West, "the father of monotheism." Without any doubt Abraham was a pure monotheist and one who truly submitted to God (that is, a true Muslim). However, he was in no way the originator of monotheism. Monotheism was the religion of Adam and was the religion of all true believers, such as Noah, between the time of Adam and Abraham. Belief in Allah alone as God and submission to Him has always been the pillar of the true religion of God.

This passage demonstrates, as well, that Abraham was not a Jew or a Christian. Abraham did not practice or submit to the Torah, which was revealed to Moses after Abraham's death.[1] Nor was Abraham one of the descendants of Judah. Obviously, Abraham also had no relation to the Christian beliefs in the Trinity. He was, simply put, a Muslim, submitting himself totally to the guidance from Allah and Allah alone. Hence, his closest connection to any people is to those people who follow the same path, which would be the Prophet Muhammad (peace and blessings of Allah be upon him) and his followers. Thus, Allah says, "Verily, among mankind who have the best claim to Abraham are those who followed him, and this Prophet [Muhammad] and those who have believed" (3:68).

Moses was also a Muslim, receiving the revelation from Allah, submitting completely to Him alone and commanding his people to

---

[1] Allah says, "O people of the Scripture (Jews and Christians)! Why do you dispute about Abraham, while the Torah and the Gospel were not revealed till after him? Have you then no sense?" (3:65).

do the same. Allah says, "Moses said, 'My people! If you do (really) believe in Allah, then in Him put your trust if you submit (your will to His)'" (10:84). Islam was also the religion of all of the prophets of the Tribes of Israel. Allah says in reference to them, "Verily, We did send down the Torah [to Moses], therein was guidance and light, by which the Prophets, who submitted themselves to Allah's Will, judged the Jews" (5:44).

Moses, for example, would have never rejected the prophethood of one of his fellow prophets, Jesus, as the Jews have done. Nor would Moses have said the types of disrespectful things about the prophet Jesus that the Jews have said.[1]

Jesus was another prophet of God who followed the religion of Islam or submitting to Allah alone. He taught this religion to his disciples. Allah says, "Then when Jesus came to know of their disbelief, he said, 'Who will be my helpers in Allah's Cause?' The disciples said, 'We are the helpers of Allah; we believe in Allah, and bear witness that we are Muslims (i.e. we submit to Allah)'" (3:52).

Jesus was human, like all the other prophets, and never claimed for himself any divine or semi-divine status. Even a reading of the New Testament can lead one to believe that Jesus never had anything to do with the concept of the Trinity and all the other beliefs that Christians later developed. In fact, Allah makes it clear that Jesus never asked anyone to worship him:

> And when Allah will say (on the Day of Resurrection), "O Jesus, son of Mary! Did you say unto the people, 'Worship me and my mother as two gods besides Allah?'" He will say, "Glory be to You! It was not for me to say what I had no right

---

[1] Shahak writes, "According to the Talmud, Jesus was executed by a proper rabbinical court for idolatry, inciting other Jews to idolatry and contempt of rabbinical authority. All classical Jewish sources which mention his execution are quite happy to take responsibility for it: in the Talmudic account the Romans are not even mentioned." Israel Shahak, *Jewish History, Jewish Religion: The Weight of Three Thousand Years* (London: Pluto Press, 1997), pp. 97-98. He also wrote (pp. 20-21) about Jesus' fate, "the Talmud states that his punishment in hell is to be immersed in boiling excrement."

(to say). Had I said such a thing, You would surely have known it. You know what is in my inner-self though I do not know what is in Yours, truly, You, only You, are the All-Knower of all that is hidden and unseen. Never did I say to them aught except what You (Allah) did command me to say: 'Worship Allah, my Lord and your Lord.' And I was a witness over them while I dwelt amongst them, but when You took me up, You were the Watcher over them, and You are a Witness to all things. If You punish them, they are Your slaves, and if You forgive them, verily You, only You are the All-Mighty, the All-Wise" (5:116-118).

Thus, the brotherhood of Islam and the bond of true faith stretches all the way from Adam until the end of time, spanning all localities and peoples. The true believers love one another and support one another. It is truly a blessed and unique brotherhood.

In particular, the true Muslims throughout all the ages believe in all of the prophets. They support all of them and defend their honor as well. This role of defending the honor of the prophets has truly fallen upon the shoulders of the followers of the Prophet Muhammad in particular today. The peoples of other faiths seem to have no qualms speaking badly about or even ridiculing their own prophets, not to speak of prophets that they reject. It seems as though it is only the followers of Muhammad today who are willing to stand and defend the honor of those noble prophets and believers. One would never hear a pious Muslim ever speak badly about Abraham, Isaac, Moses, Jesus or any of the prophets. Instead, the Muslim respects, honors and loves them *all* in the manner they deserve.

Islam: The Religion of the Prophet Muhammad

It has been shown that Islam—or the pure submission to and worship of Allah alone—was the religion of all the true prophets and believers since the time of Adam. However, after the coming of the

Prophet Muhammad (peace and blessings of Allah be upon him), there is a further distinction that needs to be made.

Before the time of the Prophet (peace and blessings of Allah be upon him), one could say that there were many "Islams." That is, each people had their prophets, followed their teachings and were on the path of Islam. At the same time, if a new prophet in the same line of prophets came to them, they had no choice but to follow that new prophet. As was discussed earlier, the one who refuses to accept Allah's later prophet is not truly submitting to Allah. If he is not truly submitting to Allah, then he is not a "Muslim."

Therefore, after the time of the Prophet Muhammad (peace and blessings of Allah be upon him) there is only one acceptable manner of worshipping and submitting to God: The path of the Prophet Muhammad. That is the only path that today can truly be called "submitting oneself to the will of Allah." Anyone who knowingly rejects the Prophet Muhammad (peace and blessings of Allah be upon him), no matter how many other prophets he believes in, is no longer submitting to God and is not a Muslim.

It is interesting to note that the only religion that has kept the name "submission to Allah" or Islam is that of the final Prophet Muhammad (peace and blessings of Allah be upon him). The other well-known religions are all named after individuals, peoples or places. According to *Microsoft Encarta*, the term Judaism did not even exist in pre-modern Hebrew. It is in reference to Judah. Christianity is, of course, named after Christ as Buddhism is named after Buddha. Hinduism has to do with the place, Hindustan. But, by Allah's wisdom and mercy, the name of the only true religion of submission to Allah—the religion of all the prophets—has been preserved and kept only in reference to the mission of the final prophet who was sent for all of humanity.[1]

---

[1] In the 1800s and early 1900s, it was common for missionaries and Orientalists to refer to Islam as Mohamedanism and to Muslims as Mohamedans. They were giving this religion a name in the same way that they had names for their own religions. But such is not acceptable for Islam and the use of these terms has, for the most part, been successfully

In sum, today, the only option left to be on the path of Islam and follow the way of all of the earlier prophets is by following the Prophet Muhammad. The Prophet's own words regarding Moses have already been quoted: "If my brother Moses were alive today, he would have no option but to follow me."[1]

The invitation is open for everyone to follow the way of the Prophet Muhammad (peace and blessings of Allah be upon him). In a beautiful statement, the Prophet explained in a parable the nature of his call to all of humankind. The Prophet explained that some angels came to him while he was sleeping. Some of the angels said, "He is sleeping [therefore leave him]." The others answered, "His eyes sleep but his heart is alert." They said, "Your companion is like this" and they propounded a similitude. They said, "His similitude is like a person who builds a house and provides a table spread filled with provisions and calls the other people to it. Those who respond to his call enter the house and eat from the table spread. Those who do not respond to his call do not enter the house nor do they eat from the table spread." Some of the angels said, "Give him its interpretation." Others replied, "He is sleeping." They were answered by others who said, "His eyes sleep but his heart is alert." So they explained the parable to him, saying, "The house is Paradise and the one inviting is Muhammad (peace be upon him). Whoever obeys Muhammad (peace be upon him) has verily obeyed Allah. Whoever disobeys Muhammad (peace be upon him) has verily disobeyed Allah. And Muhammad (peace be upon him) is a separator of humanity."[2]

In another statement, the Prophet said, "All of my people whom I am addressing [with my message] will enter Paradise except those who refuse." His companions asked, "Who would refuse?" He answered, "Whoever obeys me will enter Paradise; whoever disobeys

---

squashed. In reality, such terms are actually an affront to the religion as Muslims do not worship Muhammad in any way.

[1] Recorded by Ahmad and al-Daarimi.

[2] Recorded by al-Bukhari.

me has refused (to enter Paradise)."[1] It is as simple as that: there are those who simply refuse to follow the Prophet and, unfortunately for them, they will have to face the consequences of their choice.

But, again, this invitation is open to everyone. It is the invitation to come to the soundest statement: There is none worthy of worship except God. If others refuse, then they should bear witness that the Muslims have decided to submit to God alone. Thus, Allah says, "Say (O Muhammad), 'O people of the Scripture (Jews and Christians): Come to a word that is just between us and you, that we worship none but Allah, and that we associate no partners with Him, and that none of us shall take others as lords besides Allah. Then, if they turn away, say, 'Bear witness that we are Muslims'" (3:65).

Islam and "Religion"

Before concluding this discussion concerning the definition of the word Islam, a note is called for concerning the word and conception of "religion." The word "religion" needs to be contrasted with the Arabic word *deen*, as Islam is described throughout the Quran as a *deen*.

Many times the word "religion" is used in a quite restrictive sense. It pertains, for example, to one's beliefs about God. It usually covers some rites of worship that someone may practice. It may also reflect some ethical values and a limited amount of moral conduct. For many, though, there remains much of their lives that remain outside of the realm of religion. In other words, to them, religion is not about a "complete way of life," wherein all the aspects of his life are to be guided by the principles or teachings of the religion.

Some dictionary definitions for the English word "religion" are as follows:

1. Action or conduct indicating a belief in, reverence for, and desire to please, a divine ruling power, the exercise or practice of rites or observances implying this (*Oxford English Dictionary*).

2. Recognition on the part of man of some higher unseen power as having control of his destiny, and as being entitled to

---

[1] Recorded by al-Bukhari.

obedience, reverence, and worship, the general mental and moral attitude resulting from this belief, with reference to its effect upon the individual or the community, personal or general acceptance of this feeling as a standard of spiritual and practical life (*Oxford English Dictionary*).

3. beliefs and worship: people's beliefs and opinions concerning the existence, nature, and worship of a deity or deities, and divine involvement in the universe and human life (*Microsoft Encarta*).

4. particular system: a particular institutionalized or personal system of beliefs and practices relating to the divine (*Microsoft Encarta*).

5. personal beliefs or values: a set of strongly-held beliefs, values, and attitudes that somebody lives by (*Microsoft Encarta*).

Although some seem to come close, none of these definitions give the complete picture of what a *deen* is. In other words, Islam is something more than the impression one gets from all of these definitions of the word "religion." This author fears that when the reader thinks of Islam as a "religion", he may put it into one of these definitions and therefore may not appreciate the entire meaning of the word Islam. Thus, a more detailed discussion is necessary.

The word *deen* actually has many components to its original meaning.[1] Maududi has attempted to summarize them all into one comprehensive passage,

> [From its semantic meanings, it means] a whole
> way of life in which a person gives his submission
> and obedience to someone whom he regards as
> having the ultimate authority, shapes his conduct
> according to the bounds and laws and rules
> prescribed by that being, looks to him for

---

[1] According to Izutsu, "We must begin by admitting that it is one of the most difficult Qur'anic key-terms to handle semantically." Toshihiko Izutsu, *God and Man in the Quran: Semantics of the Quranic Weltanshauung* (Kuala Lumpur, Malaysia: Islamic Book Trust, 2002), p. 240.

recognition, honour, and reward for loyal service, and fears the disgrace or punishment that could follow any lack on his part. There is perhaps no word in the terminology of any country or people— other than Muslims—which would comprehensively embrace all factors.[1]

Note that none of the above quoted definitions for religion explicitly state that religion encompasses every moment and aspect of one's life, which is captured in the concept of *deen*. If, for example, the last definition were adjusted, it would be virtually correct: "a set of strongly-held beliefs, values, and attitudes that somebody lives by *encompassing all of the aspects of his life.*" Thus, it also encompasses all aspects of social interaction and therefore goes beyond, "personal beliefs or values" as given in fifth definition above.

Second, some of these definitions are lacking with respect to the concepts of obedience and servitude, concepts essential to the term *deen*.[2] The second definition captures part of this: "Recognition on the part of man of some higher unseen power…as being entitled to obedience, reverence, and worship." This definition would further be improved by changing "obedience" to "absolute obedience."

Third, important to the word *deen* is also the acceptance of the divine authority and therefore the willingness and understanding that submission to Him is right and proper. In other words, the individual recognizes that this relationship is correct and therefore wants to fulfill his part of the relationship. The first definition almost captures this concept: "indicating a belief in, reverence for, and desire to please."[3]

Although these points may be throughout the different definitions of religion given above, they all have to be captured in the

---

[1] Abul Ala Maududi, *Four Basic Quranic Terms* (Lahore, Pakistan: Islamic Publications, Ltd., 2000), pp. 99-100.

[2] Cf., Izutsu, p. 240.

[3] Note that the first definition then reduces the matter to the practice of rites or observances, which is insufficient.

one definition of the Arabic word *deen*. In other words, they all have to be present in the understanding of Islam as a "religion."

In sum, *deen*, in its religious sense, means willfully giving up oneself to the absolute authority of God with complete and devoted servitude and obedience in all realms of life, embodying all laws coming from God, recognizing that this is God's deserved right and realizing that this is one's noble purpose. This is what "religion" or *deen* is from an Islamic perspective and this is what is expected from the Muslim.

The Foundation and Sources of Islam

There are only two absolute sources of Islam: the Quran and the Sunnah of the Prophet Muhammad (peace and blessings of Allah be upon him). These two are the absolute sources in Islam because they constitute the revelation received by the Prophet (peace and blessings of Allah be upon him) from God. God inspired the Prophet with both the Quran and the Sunnah. Hence, all beliefs and practices are subservient to these foundations: if something is consistent with them, it may be accepted; if something contradicts them, it must be rejected.

The miraculous nature as well as the preservation of the Quran were touched upon earlier. Much more, though, can be said about the Quran.

The Quran is very different from the Bible. The Quran does not consist of stories told by humans about different prophets, every so often actually quoting a prophet. The Quran is actually the word of God. It was revealed by God, via the angel Gabriel, directly to the Prophet Muhammad (peace and blessings of Allah be upon him). The Prophet received the exact wording and passed it on to his followers. This revelation, with its exact wording, was memorized, recorded and passed on as is. Hence, again, it is God and only God speaking in the Quran. There are no comments, passages or quotes from humans whatsoever in the Quran.

The style of the Quran is therefore unique. It is Allah's words to the heart, mind and soul of humans. It moves from one topic to another in fascinating fashion. It even changes between first, second and third person, sometimes putting words into the reader's own mouth. It moves smoothly from descriptions of God to laws about inheritance, food and so forth—always reminding in the end that the ultimate goal is to be dutiful to Allah. In its original language of Arabic, it is extremely moving and beautiful. (Today, the "meaning" of the Quran has been translated into numerous languages. However, none of these translations is ever considered the Quran.[1] The Quran is only the Arabic original. Hence, in the prayers and rituals, only the true, original Arabic Quran is used.)

The entire Quran was not revealed to the Prophet all at once. Instead, it was revealed bit by bit over a period of twenty-three years.[2] It guided the early Muslim community along every step it took. It thus completely transformed that community into a pious generation. In the meantime, it set examples for all later Muslim communities who will face some of the same circumstances they faced. It transformed an Arab people who were on the margins of the civilized world at that time into the leaders of a great civilization, whose influence still continues today. When read, understood and applied properly today, it will also transform individuals or society and exalt them to new heights of piety and closeness to God.

In addition to the Quran, there are the sayings and example of the Prophet Muhammad (peace and blessings of Allah be upon him). As noted earlier, the authority of the Sunnah of the Messenger of

---

[1] Muhammad Marmaduke Pickthall was the first Western Muslim to translate the Quran into English. In his introduction he wrote, "Although I have sought to present an almost-literal and appropriate rendering worthy of the Arabic original, I cannot reproduce its inimitable symphony, the very sounds of which move men to tears and ecstasy. This present volume represents only an attempt to present the meaning and some of the charm of the Qur'an in English. It can never take the place of the original Arabic Qur'an, nor is it meant to do so." Muhammad Marmaduke Pickthall, trans., *The Glorious Quran* (New York: Muslim World League, n.d.), p. iii.

[2] One of the miraculous aspects of the Quran is its internal consistency. Although it was revealed over a period of twenty-three years, it contains no contradictions or discrepancies. In fact, Allah even says, "Do they not then ponder the Quran carefully? Had it been from other than Allah, they would surely have found therein many discrepancies" (4:82).

Allah is not because he is some kind of demigod. He was a human being, just like all of the other prophets. The prophet's authority is related to the issue of submission to Allah: It is Allah in the Quran who establishes the authority of the Prophet. Hence, following the way of the Prophet is nothing but acting in obedience and submission to Allah. Allah has virtually said such when He said, "He who obeys the Messenger has indeed obeyed Allah, but he who turns away, then we have not sent you (O Muhammad) as a watcher over them" (4:80).

In the Quran, Allah makes it clear that if someone loves Allah and wishes that Allah should love him in return, the key is to follow the way of the Prophet Muhammad (peace and blessings of Allah be upon him). Allah says, "Say (O Muhammad to humankind), 'If you (truly) love Allah then follow me, Allah will love you and forgive you of your sins. And Allah is Oft-Forgiving, Most Merciful'" (3:31).

The Quran says about the Prophet, "Indeed in the Messenger of Allah you have an excellent example to follow for him who hopes in (the Meeting with) Allah and the Last Day and remembers Allah much" (33:21). The Prophet was, in a way, a "living Quran." When the Prophet's wife Aishah was asked about his character and behavior, she replied, "His character was the Quran."[1]

There is a very important relationship between the Quran and the Sunnah. The Sunnah demonstrates how the Quran is to be implemented. It is a practical explanation of what the Quran is teaching. It defines the morals, behaviors and laws of the Quran in such a way that its meaning becomes clear. As mentioned earlier, this complete, human embodiment of the teachings of the Quran is a great blessing and mercy for Muslims. It makes the guidance from God more complete and accessible to all.

Thus, the Quran and the Sunnah form one united unit that offer all the principles of guidance that humankind will need until the Day of Judgment.

---

[1] Recorded by Muslim.

The Levels of the Faith

In a famous hadith, the Angel Gabriel, with the intent of teaching the people their faith, asked the Prophet Muhammad (peace and blessings of Allah be upon him) some questions. A portion of that hadith reads as follows:

> [The Angel Gabriel] said, "O Muhammad, tell me about Islam." The Messenger of Allah (peace be upon him) said, "Islam is to testify that there is none worthy of worship except Allah and that Muhammad is the Messenger of Allah, to establish the prayers, to pay the zakat, to fast [the month of] Ramadhan, and to make the pilgrimage to the House if you have the means to do so." He said, "You have spoken truthfully [or correctly]." We were amazed that he asks the question and then he says that he had spoken truthfully. He said, "Tell me about *Imaan* (faith)." He [the Messenger of Allah (peace be upon him)] responded, "It is to believe in Allah, His angels, His books, His messengers, the Last Day and to believe in the divine decree, [both] the good and the evil thereof."
> He said, "You have spoken truthfully." He said, "Tell me about *al-Ihsaan* (goodness)…"[1]

This hadith highlights the third usage of the term Islam: the outward act of submitting to Allah as opposed to the inward acts of faith. Based on this hadith, it can be seen that there are three levels of "faith" or "religiousness": "Islam," "faith" and "*ihsaan*." Each deserves to be discussed separately.

The Level of "Islam"

When juxtaposed with "faith," Islam (submission) refers to the outwards acts of submission or, in other words, the actual deeds that one performs.

---

[1] Recorded by Muslim.

In answering the question from the Angel Gabriel, the Prophet listed some acts of submission. Obviously, these are not the only acts of submission. In fact, every good deed performed with the intention of pleasing God and in accord with His revelation is an act of submission. However, the specific acts mentioned by the Prophet in this hadith have a special role. They are commonly referred to as the "five pillars of Islam." In fact, in another hadith, the Prophet Muhammad stated, "Islam is built upon five [pillars]: testifying that there is none worthy of worship except Allah and that Muhammad is the Messenger of Allah, establishing the prayers, giving the zakat, making the pilgrimage to the House and fasting the month of Ramadhan."[1]

As this author has written elsewhere,

> Here, the Messenger of Allah (peace be upon him) has given a parable in which he gives a picture of Islam like that of a house. The foundations or pillars of the house are five. If the house is missing these five, then, in reality, it does not exist at all. The other acts of Islam are like complementary parts or parts that add to the completeness of the house. If any of the complementary parts are missing, the house is still standing but it has a deficiency; it is not complete or perfect. However, if all of the pillars are missing, the house will not be standing or in existence at all. In particular, if the main pillar is missing[2], the house cannot stand or be said to exist.[3]

In this section, a brief description of the five pillars is given while later some of the long-term benefits of these acts will be discussed.

---

[1] Recorded by al-Bukhari and Muslim.

[2] The main pillar is the testimony of faith.

[3] Jamaal Zarabozo, *Commentary on the Forty Hadith of al-Nawawi* (Boulder, CO: al-Basheer Company for Publications and Translations, 1998), vol. 1, p. 335.

The first pillar is the proclamation of faith. This first pillar demonstrates that submission is not something that one claims is in the heart with no public affirmation. The submission to God is not meant to be a private submission. It is a public submission, as it is the driving force behind the outward deeds one performs. Thus, with full conviction, belief, sincerity and honesty one proclaims: There is none worthy of worship except Allah and Muhammad is the messenger of Allah.

In reality, without this pillar, the remaining acts will become meaningless. The other acts must be built upon having faith. One cannot do an act to please God properly without first having belief in God and in His Messenger. This faith then drives corresponding acts. The first act that this faith should lead one to is the proclamation and declaration of that faith. Hence, it is the starting point for all of the other foundations.

The second pillar is "to establish the prayers." This pillar does not simply mean to pray whenever or however one wills to pray. There are formal, ritualistic prayers that every Muslim must perform as a basic sign of his willingness to submit to God.[1] There are five such prayers every day at fixed times. The time of the first prayer is between dawn and sunrise. The second prayer time starts just after high noon. The third starts at the mid-afternoon. The fourth starts right after sunset. And the fifth is at nightfall. Hence, as a Muslim goes through his day there is never any period of time in which he is distant from a formal prayer. These repeated prayers continually remind the person of his relationship with his Lord and his true purpose in life.

In general, these prayers are supposed to be performed in congregation in a mosque. Numerous mosques are therefore located throughout Muslim lands. The faithful are called to pray by a person reciting specific phrases, among them, "Come to the prayer, come to the success." In the mosque, the worshippers form straight lines

---

[1] Obviously, one can pray or supplicate at all times and perform voluntary prayers on one's own. However, this is not what this foundational pillar is referring to.

behind the prayer leader (Imam). They all face the same direction, towards Mecca. The prayer is said in Arabic and contains Quranic readings. The prayer also consists of bows and prostrations. If anyone travels throughout the world, he will find the Muslims praying in the same fashion and with the same Arabic terms and expressions. Thus, a Muslim enters any mosque in the world and feels immediately at home and among his brothers and sisters in faith. There is no need to look for a "Vietnamese-American mosque[1]" or a "German mosque" or anything of that nature. Everyone knows how the prayer is going be performed, everyone understands what is happening and everyone prays together no matter what his background, social status, race and so forth. Actually, everyone is going to pray in the same manner in which the Prophet Muhammad himself prayed. (Since one knows that this is the manner in which the Prophet prayed, one can be fully satisfied that it is a manner which is pleasing to Allah.)

The prayers are a type of purification for a human being. He turns and meets with his Lord five times a day. As alluded to above, this repeated standing in front of Allah should keep the person from performing sins during the day. Furthermore, it should also be a time of remorse and repentance, such that he earnestly asks Allah for forgiveness for those sins that he committed. In addition, the prayer in itself is a good deed that wipes away some of the evil deeds that he performed. These points can be noted in the following hadith of the Prophet (peace be upon him): "If a person had a stream outside his door and he bathed in it five times a day, do you think he would have any filth left on him?" The people said, "No filth would remain on him whatsoever." The Prophet (peace be upon him) then said, "That is like the five daily prayers: Allah wipes away the sins by them."[2]

For many Muslim scholars, the ritual prayers are the minimum ritual act of worship expected of a Muslim.[3] If someone is

---

[1] One can find churches of this nature scattered throughout the United States.

[2] Recorded by al-Bukhari and Muslim.

[3] In fact, the Prophet himself said, "Between a person and idolatry and disbelief is the leaving of the prayer." (Recorded by Muslim.)

not even willing to perform these prayers daily, it cannot be said of him that he is willing to truly submit to Allah. Hence, he cannot be considered a true Muslim.

The third pillar of Islam is the paying of *zakat* or "alms." Lexically, the root of the word zakat implies purification, blessing and growth. Another word used in the Quran and hadith for the zakat is *sadaqa*. This word is derived from *sidq* (truthfulness). Siddiqi explains the significance of these two terms as they used here,

> Both these words are highly meaningful. The spending of wealth for the sake of Allah purifies the heart of man of the love of material wealth. The man who spends it offers that as a humble gift before the Lord and thus affirms the truth that nothing is dearer to him in life than the love of Allah and that he is fully prepared to sacrifice everything for His sake.[1]

In Islamic Law, the technical meaning of *zakat* is in reference to a specific portion of one's varied wealth that must be given yearly to a specific group of recipients, such as the poor and the needy.

In Islam, righteousness is not restricted to one's own individual heartfelt feelings or personal worship. Righteousness must also spread to others in the community and even to the world as a whole. The *zakat* makes the individual realize that he is not an island unto himself. Instead, each individual is actually a member of a society—in particular, a member of an Islamic brotherhood. The different members of this society have rights and responsibilities with respect to one another. The proper interaction with others in society is actually part of one's worship of God.

Zakat also reminds the individual that the wealth that he possesses is actually a bounty from Allah. When it comes to the distribution of wealth in the world today, much of it is dependent on what people would call "luck," such as being born into the right family, living at the right time and place and stumbling upon

---

[1] Siddiqi, vol. 2, p. 465.

excellent opportunities. This is not "luck" but these are all different aspects that Allah has decreed for each individual. Hence, one has to be grateful to Allah and be willing to give some of the wealth that Allah has bestowed upon him.

The fourth pillar of Islam is the fast of the nine month of the Islamic calendar, Ramadhan. This means to abstain from food, drink and sexual intercourse during the daytime—from dawn until sunset—of the days of this month.[1]

Fasting is a source of self-restraint, piety and God-consciousness. It was prescribed by Allah for the prophets before Prophet Muhammad (peace be upon him). In the verses obligating the fast of the month of Ramadhan, Allah has pointed out its goal or purpose: "O you who believe! Observing the fast is prescribed for you as it was prescribed for those before you, that you may become pious" (2:183).

Note that fasting is much more than simply restraining from food, drink and sexual intercourse. It is supposed to be a time in which God-consciousness is greatly heightened. This increased level of God-consciousness should be reflected in everything the individual does while fasting. The Prophet (peace and blessings of Allah be upon him) alluded to this fact when he stated, "Perhaps the fasting person may get nothing from his fast except hunger. And perhaps the one who performs the late night prayers[2] may get nothing from his prayers except sleeplessness."[3] The Prophet (peace and blessings of Allah be upon him) also said, "The fasting is [not only abstaining] from food and drink but the fast is abstaining from vain speech and

---

[1] Note that the Islamic calendar is a lunar calendar. Hence, over the years, the month of Ramadhan moves throughout the different seasons. In any given year, those in the Northern Hemisphere may be fasting during summer (with relatively longer days) while those in the Southern Hemisphere are fasting during winter (relatively shorter days). However, in a number of years, the situation will be reversed.

[2] In addition to fasting during the daytime, there are also special prayers that Muslims perform during the nighttime in the month of Ramadhan.

[3] Recorded by ibn Majah. Authenticated by al-Albani. See al-Albani, *Sahih al-Jami al-Sagheer*, vol. 1, p. 656, hadith #3488.

lewd speech. If anyone reviles you or acts foolishly with you, you should say, 'I am fasting, I am fasting.'"[1] Finally, the Prophet (peace and blessings of Allah be upon him) also said, "If someone does not give up false speech and acting according to it, Allah is in no want of him giving up his food and drink."[2]

The next pillar of Islam mentioned in this narration of this hadith is making the pilgrimage (*hajj*) to the House of Allah, or the Kaaba. In Islamic Law, it means traveling to Mecca in the last month of the Islamic calendar for the purpose of worshipping Allah alone. The pilgrimage should be made at least once in a Muslim's lifetime if he ever has the physical and financial means to perform it.

Part of the pilgrimage has to do with remembrance of the acts of Abraham, his wife Hagar and their son Ishmael in the valley of Mecca. One virtually retraces some of their steps. One remembers them as they sacrificed for the sake of Allah and Allah, in return, was pleased with them and blessed them in so many ways.

The pilgrimage is truly a moving experience. Millions of Muslims come from every corner of the world and descend upon Mecca. They all repeatedly express their willingness to come to be in the service of the Lord. The worldly distinctions between the pilgrims disappear as they all stand before their Lord during these blessed days. Siddiqi describes the significance of Hajj in the following manner,

> It is rightly said that it [the Hajj] is the perfection of faith since it combines in itself all the distinctive qualities of other obligatory acts. It represents the quality of *salat* [prayer] since a pilgrim offers prayers in the Kaba, the House of the Lord. It encourages spending of material wealth for the sake of the Lord, the chief characteristic of Zakat. When a pilgrim sets out for Hajj, he dissociates himself

---

[1] Recorded by al-Hakim and al-Baihaqi. Authenticated by al-Albani. See al-Albani, *Sahih al-Jami al-Sagheer*, vol. 2, p. 948, hadith #5376.
[2] Recorded by al-Bukhari.

from his hearth and home, from his dear and near ones to please the Lord. He suffers privation and undertakes the hardship of journey— the lessons we learn from fasting and *itikaf*.[1] In Hajj one is trained to be completely forgetful of the material comforts and pomp and show of worldly life. One has to sleep on stony ground[2], circumambulate the Kaba, run between Safa and Marwa[3] and spend his night and day wearing only two pieces of unsewn cloth. He is required to avoid the use of oil or scent or any other perfume. He is not even allowed to get his hair cut or trim his beard. In short, he is commanded to abandon everything for the sake of Allah and submit himself before his Lord, the ultimate aim of the life of a Muslim. In fact, physical pilgrimage is a prelude to spiritual pilgrimage to God, when man would bid goodbye to everything of the world and present himself before Him as His humble servant saying: "Here I am before Thee, my Lord, as a slave of Thine."[4]

As noted earlier, these acts form the foundation of one's overall life of submission to Allah. Building upon what one learns from these ritual acts, one becomes a complete servant of Allah in every realm of life.

---

[1] *Itikaf* is where one secludes himself in the mosque for personal worship and devotion. Most commonly, this is done at the end of the month of Ramadhan.

[2] This is not a must but it is how many pilgrims spend their nights. Today, though, most people stay in tents or hotels.

[3] These are two hillocks that Hagar raced back and forth between while seeking water for her son Ishmael. The angel eventually uncovered a well for her, known as the well of Zamzam. To this day, that well continues to pour forth water for the millions of pilgrims who come to Mecca every year.

[4] Siddiqi, vol. 2, p. 577. The last statement he made is very close to what the pilgrims chant during the pilgrimage.

The Level of *Imaan* ("Faith")

In addition to outward submission, one must also have faith in one's heart. On this issue, two points are very important. The first is concerned with what one is supposed to believe in or, in other terms, the articles of faith. The second has to do with what transformations should take place when this faith in the heart is truly the overriding force in one's life.

The Angel Gabriel said to the Prophet, "Tell me about *Imaan* (faith)." He [the Messenger of Allah (peace be upon him)] responded, "It is to believe in Allah, His angels, His books, His messengers, the Last Day and to believe in the divine decree, [both] the good and the evil thereof." Hence, in this hadith, the Prophet is mentioning the primary articles of faith. These articles are six in number as follows:

(1) Belief in Allah: Belief in Allah is the cornerstone of Islamic faith. This article of faith has been explained throughout this work and needs no further elaboration here.

(2) Belief in the Angels: Angels are a type of creation of Allah that is, in general, unseen by man. They have been created from light but they do have forms and bodies. They are servants of Allah and have no aspect of divinity to them whatsoever. They submit to His command completely and never stray from fulfilling His orders. The fact that there are some types of beings beyond the realm of human experience should not be shocking. As Tabbarah noted, "Every day science discovers living creatures which we had no idea about before. This leads us to ask: Were these creatures non-existent before their discovery, and have they started to exist the moment man discovered them?"[1]

(3) Belief in the Books revealed by Allah: Belief in Allah's books refers to the revelations that Allah sent down to His messengers as a mercy and guidance to lead mankind to success in this life and happiness in the Hereafter. The Quran refers to a number of such books: the scrolls of Abraham, the Torah of Moses, the Psalms of David and the Gospel of Jesus. (It must be recalled that the

---

[1] Tabbarah, p. 87.

original revelations that these prophets received are not the same as the books that go under such names today. They were not preserved properly.) Belief in the books also includes belief in the Quran as the final revelation. It is very important to realize that it is considered the height of arrogance and a form of disbelief for an individual to declare for himself the right to believe in portions of what Allah revealed and reject other portions of it. Thus, Allah says, "Then do you believe in a part of the Scripture and reject the rest? Then what is the recompense of those who do so among you, except disgrace in the life of this world, and on the Day of Resurrection they shall be consigned to the most grievous torment. And Allah is not unaware of what you do" (2:85).

(4) Belief in the Messengers: This concept has also been discussed in detail earlier and needs no further elaboration.

(5) Belief in the Last Day and the Resurrection: "The Last Day" is called such because there will be no new day after it, as the people of Paradise shall be in their abode as will the people of Hell. Its other names include "The Day of Resurrection," "The Reality," "The Event," "The Day of Judgment," and "The Overwhelming." This is the greatest day that humankind shall pass through. Indeed, it will be the gravest and most fearful day. A person's new life will be decided on that day. It will mark a new beginning for each soul. This new step may lead to eternal bliss or eternal damnation. Belief in the Last Day implies belief in everything that the Quran or the Prophet (peace be upon him) has stated about the events of that Day and thereafter. There are some general aspects (resurrection, judgment and reward, Paradise and Hell) as well as more detailed aspects that the Quran or the Messenger of Allah (peace be upon him) mentioned. The more one has knowledge of that Day and its surrounding events, the greater the affect this belief will have on him. Hence, the Quran and Sunnah provide great detail as to the events of that Day and time.

It is important to realize that no one can say for certain who will be in Paradise or Hell.[1] Nobody knows what will happen to any

---

[1] Unless, of course, such has been explicitly stated in the Quran or the Sunnah.

individual. A righteous person today may change and become impious tomorrow, leading himself to Hell. The greatest enemy of Islam and disbeliever may repent in the future and become the most pious of people, leading himself to Heaven. In fact, there are some who may never hear about Islam or have only been offered a very distorted picture of Islam. Only God knows what will happen to such people in the Hereafter. However, some things are certain: God alone will be the judge on the Day of Judgment, God will never wrong any soul even the slightest amount and if a person is a true Muslim and believer, Allah will be pleased with him.

(6) Belief in the Divine Decree (*al-Qadar*): This refers to belief in the fact that nothing can occur in this creation except by the will and permission of Allah. There is no power that can go against His will. He has control over all things. This does not mean, though, that Islam is fatalistic. Humans have been given a type of free will. However, Allah, with His perfect knowledge, has foreknowledge of what humans will do. He has knowledge of what they will do and He wills it and decrees it but He does not cause them to make their life choices. Jaafar Sheikh Idris has adequately dealt with one of the sources of confusion on this point. He wrote,

> "If our actions are willed by God," someone might say, "then they are in fact His actions." This objection is based on a confusion. God wills what we will in the sense of granting us the will to choose and enabling us to execute that will, i.e., He creates all that makes it possible for us to do it. He does not will it in the sense of doing it, otherwise it would be quite in order to say, when we drink or eat or sleep for instance, that God performed these actions. God creates them, He does not do or perform them. Another objection, based on another confusion, is that if God allows us to do evil, then He approves of it and likes it. But to will something in the sense of allowing a person to do it is one

thing; and to approve of his action and commend it is quite another...[1]

The above are the six articles of faith in the Muslim religion. There is an important second issue related to "faith": What does *imaan* or "faith" really mean for a person and what are its implications? First, faith, meaning true and definitive belief in something, should lead to a corresponding submission to what one believes in. Otherwise, it is simply an acceptance of a fact but it is not the Islamic concept of "faith" (*imaan*). Thus, Ibn Uthaimin wrote,

> *Imaan* is the affirmation that requires acceptance and submission. If a person believes in something without acceptance and submission, that is not *imaan*. The evidence for that is that the polytheists [Arabs] believed in Allah's existence and believed in Allah as the Creator, Sustainer, Giver of Life, Bringer of Death and the Manager of the Universe's Affairs. Furthermore, one of them even accepted the messengership of the Prophet Muhammad (peace be upon him) but he was not a believer. That person was Abu Talib, the uncle of the Prophet (peace be upon him)... But that [belief in the Prophet (peace be upon him)] will not avail him whatsoever because he did not accept and submit to what the Prophet (peace be upon him) brought.[2]

A person's beliefs are the most important aspect of his being. They are, in general, the driving forces behind his way of life and personal choices. The true and effective beliefs never remain at an abstract level but their influence is manifested on a day-to-day practical level. In other words, there is no true "faith" or *imaan*

---

[1] Jaafar Sheikh Idris, *The Pillars of Faith* (Riyadh: Presidency of Islamic Research, Ifta and Propagation, 1984), pp. 26-27.

[2] Muhammad ibn Uhtaimin, *Sharh Hadith Jibreel Alaihi al-Salaam* (Dar al-Thuraya, 1415 A.H.), pp. 4-5.

without that having a strong influence upon a person's act. A person cannot claim, "I have belief in my heart," yet, at the same time, that person never actually does acts of worship. This person's actions are belying his claim of "faith in the heart."

Thus, true faith has to influence the person's deeds. To take a simple example, the question of cheating and stealing is directly related to one's overall belief system. If a person believes that these acts are morally wrong and that there is an all-knowing, just God who will hold him accountable for his deeds, he will most likely refrain from such acts. But if a person does not believe in any eternal ramifications or any day of judgment or if his heart is not affected by such feelings, his deciding factor may only be the chances of being caught and the severity of the punishment for those acts.

When the heart is filled with *Imaan*—a concept which also includes the love of Allah, fear of Allah, hope in Allah— it will drive the body to perform acts of obedience and keep away from forbidden acts. Hence, in reality, there is no such thing as true or strong *Imaan* being in the heart and that not being reflected in the deeds.

But this feeling in the heart is not a static and fixed thing. There is no such thing as, "I accepted faith on such and such day and I am a complete believer now and forever." Actually, the level of faith, as reflecting in the real effects of such faith, is constantly increasing or decreasing. Many factors influence "faith" or *imaan*. Perhaps every individual has experienced this. At times, a person is very aware of God and of his fear and love for Him. This strong feeling in the person's heart brings tranquility and warmth to the person and it also keeps him from committing sins. However, at other times, perhaps when the affairs of this world are engulfing him, his remembrance and attachment to Allah is not that great. He does not feel that great feeling of faith in his heart. His behavior and actions are not of the same quality as they are at other times. When he encounters this stage, his soul becomes too tired or not willing to sacrifice. This is nothing but the fluctuations of *Imaan* in the person's heart. It is clear that these fluctuations in turn affect the actions that a person performs.

At times, therefore, a person may continue to be a Muslim, in the general sense of the word as one who is submitting to God and not recognizing any other god, but the influence of his faith is weak upon him. He is not deserving of being called a "true believer" although he certainly has not lost all faith. It is in states like this where one commits sins, sometimes even major sins. Thus, the Prophet (peace and blessings of Allah be upon him) said, "A fornicator while committing illegal sexual intercourse is not a [true] believer. A thief while committing theft is not a [true] believer. A drinker while drinking alcohol is not a [true] believer."[1] When the person realizes what has happened to his faith, he should repent to God, rebuild his faith and strive to be a better believer.

Everyone should keep in mind the fact that faith increases and decreases. Hence, the believer should always be on the lookout for any sign that his faith is decreasing. Indeed, he should take positive steps to increase his faith. This would include such things as reading the Quran, remembering Allah, pondering over the creation and so forth—actions that will help one revive and increase one's faith. In fact, increasing one's knowledge about Allah, the Prophet (peace and blessings of Allah be upon him) and Islam is one of the greatest means to increase one's faith.

It is very important for new Muslims to realize that faith increases and decreases. When a person first embraces Islam, he has taken the step of submitting to Allah. At the same time, though, he may not have the knowledge needed to make his heart full of conviction or he may not have the kind of love for Allah that puts Allah above everything else in his life. He may still have some remnants in his heart and mind that actually contradict Islam. However, as he grows in Islam, his *imaan* will also grow, Allah willing. He will become more certain of Islam's truth, more dedicated

---

[1] Recorded by al-Bukhari and Muslim.

to Allah and, eventually, his *imaan* will be the greatest driving force in his life.

There is one more level that goes beyond "believer" and this is *muhsin*, the one characterized by *ihsaan* (excellence in his worship of Allah). Every *muhsin* must meet all of the conditions of a Muslim and a believer. Hence, every *muhsin* is a Muslim and a believer. However, not every believer is a *muhsin*. Being a *muhsin* is a stage higher than that of being a *mumin* or *muslim*.

The Level of *Ihsaan*

The Angel Gabriel then said to the Prophet (peace and blessings of Allah be upon him), "Tell me about *al-Ihsaan* (goodness)." He [the Prophet] answered, "It is that you worship Allah as if you see Him. And even though you do not see Him, [you know] He sees you."

The lexical meaning of *ihsaan* implies doing well, doing goodness, behaving with others in a goodly manner. It is the opposite of causing harm to someone else. In such a case, the form of the word will be followed with a preposition. However, the word also implies perfecting something or doing something in the best way. This is, perhaps, closer to what is meant by the word *ihsaan* in this particular hadith. However, the two concepts are not inseparable. A person will behave towards others in the best way possible if he is truly doing that to please Allah. Hence, he excels both in his relation towards Allah— or rites of worship— as well as in his relationship to Allah's creatures, due to his knowledge that Allah is watching him.

Therefore, *ihsaan* is a very comprehensive term. It includes all types of acts of goodness to others. Its meaning is that a person spreads good instead of harm to others. He uses his wealth, knowledge, position and body to do good to others. He gives part of his wealth in zakat and charity, and that is *ihsaan*. He spreads his knowledge and never misses an opportunity to guide others, and that is *ihsaan* with respect to his knowledge. He uses his rightful position and influence to help those that are deserving and in need of help.

That is also *ihsaan*. He helps another person get into his car or to carry something and that is an example of *ihsaan*.

In this hadith, the Messenger of Allah (peace be upon him) did not give a dictionary-type definition of *ihsaan*. Instead, he explained the main motivating factor behind *ihsaan* or goodness and excellence. This is the fact that Allah is watching one's actions. If the heart is aware of that fact, the person will hope to please his Lord and fear displeasing Him. This will bring about purity in his heart. When such purity is present in the heart, he will do what he can for Allah's sake. This also means that he will try to do everything in the best possible way. He will be concerned about the quality of his deeds and not simply their quantity or outward execution.[1]

Ihsaan does not imply the real seeing of Allah but a very strong feeling in the heart. This is where the realization of Allah's presence, by His knowledge and mercy, is so great that the person practically witnesses Allah in front of him. The person's thought and mind become completely attuned to the act of worship or deed he is performing. This is the implication of the first sentence, "It is that you worship Allah as if you see Him." There is no question that if one could see Allah, this would have a profound effect on his worship and obedience of Allah.

The effect of the feeling of the seeing of Allah on the person is that he will perform every act of obedience in the best way possible. He practically sees Allah in front of him so he knows full well— beyond a mere theoretical belief— that Allah is observing everything that he is doing. He will be extremely shy and embarrassed to do anything in a less than perfect or excellent manner. He will also be filled with the fear, awe and admiration of Allah. He will make every effort to please Allah who he "sees" in front of him. He will exert himself to perform his act of worship in the best way possible, without any deficiency.

It is this kind of relationship with Allah that everyone should strive to possess. If a person understands what it means to

---

[1] Cf., Salaam, p. 183.

believe in Allah, the only one worthy of worship, it will fill his heart with great love for Allah and the desire to please Him in the best manner possible. He will "feel" and "experience" Allah always around him and with him. To make a worldly analogy, he will behave as if his most beloved companion is right next to him and he fears that he may do anything to hurt his feelings or bring him harm. Thus, every action is weighed and considered beforehand. If there is any shortcoming in his action, he will repent and plead for forgiveness. He will be deserving of Allah's love and pleasure as he has demonstrated that he loves Allah and wishes only to please Him.

What Humans Get From Islam

In reality, all of the benefits of Islam accrue to the human. It is solely for his own benefit that Allah has provided His guidance to humankind. Allah, Himself, is not in need of humankind's worship. He is free of all needs but in His Mercy He has shown mankind the proper mode of behavior to meet His approval. Thus, He says, "Whoever goes right, then he goes right only for the benefit of his ownself. And whoever goes astray, then he goes astray to his own loss. No one laden with burdens can bear another's burden" (17:15). In addition, it is important to note that those who reject Islam are only harming themselves. Allah says, "Truly! Allah wrongs not mankind in aught; but mankind wrong themselves" (10:44).

It would be impossible to list all of the benefits that humans get from Islam. A brief mention of some of the major issues is called for.

First and definitely most important, by following Islam the individual is following the only way of life that is pleasing to his Creator and Lord. This motivation should be so great that no other point need be made. Allah says, "And whoever seeks a religion other than Islam, it will never be accepted of him, and in the Hereafter he will be one of the losers" (3:85).

Islam is the only way of life that is truly consistent with one's own human nature, having been revealed by the One who also created the human. Thus, it is the only source for true contentment and tranquility. Islam, as Allah has described it, is a cure for all of the diseases that afflict the human's heart and soul. Those who refuse to submit to God spend their entire lives chasing after other things, many times material things, that can never bring them true happiness.

This point is not related simply to what will occur in the Hereafter. This is also something true while a person is living in this worldly life. Allah says, "Whoever works righteousness, whether male or female, while he (or she) is a true believer verily, to him We will give a good life (in this world with respect, contentment and lawful provision), and We shall pay them certainly a reward in proportion to the best of what they used to do (i.e. Paradise in the Hereafter)" (16:97). Allah also says, "But whosoever turns away from My Reminder (i.e. neither believes in this Quran nor acts on its orders, etc.) verily, for him is a life of hardship, and We shall raise him up blind on the Day of Resurrection" 20:124).

Hence, ibn al-Qayyim wrote,

> Do not consider that Allah's words, "Indeed, the righteous will be in pleasure and indeed the wicked will be in Hell-fire" [*al-Infitaar* 13-14] are restricted only to the pleasures and hell of the Hereafter alone. Actually, it applies to their [humans'] three stages, that is, the life in this world, the life in *al-barzakh* [after death and before resurrection] and the life in the permanent abode [after resurrection]. Those [who submit to God] are in pleasure while the others are in a hell. Isn't pleasure only the pleasure of the heart and punishment only the punishment of the heart? What punishment can be harsher than fear, worry, anxiety and uneasiness [faced by those who refuse to submit to God]? [What can be harsher than the soul's] turning away from Allah and the abode of

the Hereafter, its clinging on to something other than Allah and its being disconnected from Allah?[1]

Ibn Taimiyyah, a well-known scholar in the history of Islam, attempted to express the joy that one feels from his faith in Allah. He once said, "In this world there is a Paradise that whoever does not enter it will not enter the Paradise in the Hereafter." He also said, "What can my enemies do to me? Certainly, my paradise and garden are in my chest."[2] In fact, ibn al-Qayyim, ibn Taimiyyah's closest student who would visit him often, stated,

> Allah knows that I have never seen anyone having a better life than him. [This was true] even though he was in straitened circumstances and not living in luxuries and comforts. On the contrary, he was on the opposite extreme. Even though he faced imprisonment, torture and threats, he still had the most pleasurable life among the people, with the most relaxed feelings, strongest in heart and happiest of all of them. The experiencing of joy could be seen on his face. Whenever we were very fearful, feeling bad expectations and felt the earth constricting upon us, we would come to him and we only needed to see him and listen to his words that all of those emotions would leave us. Instead, we would be filled with rest, strength, certainty and tranquility. Exalted be the One who allows His servant to witness His Paradise before he meets Him.[3]

Of course, such a beautiful feeling from one's faith was not restricted to ibn Taimiyyah. Ibn al-Qayyim quotes another devout Muslim as saying, "If the kings and the children of the kings knew what

---

[1] Muhammad ibn al-Qayyim, *Al-Jawaab al-Kaafi liman Sa`ala an al-Dawaa al-Shaafi* (Beirut: Dar al-Kutub al-Ilmiyyah, 1983), p. 88-89.

[2] Quoted in Ibn al-Qayyim, *al-Waabil al-Sayyib*, p. 73.

[3] Ibn al-Qayyim, *al-Waabil al-Sayyib*, p. 73.

[felicity] we are in, they would fight us over it with their swords." Yet another stated, "The inhabitants of this world are miserable. They leave this world and they do not taste the most wonderful aspect that it contains." When asked what that was, he replied, "Love for Allah, knowing Him and remembering Him." Ibn al-Qayyim also quoted another who said, "There comes some times in which I say, 'If the people of Paradise are in a state like this, they are enjoying a good life.'"[1]

Finally, the individual will be able to experience the truest and most enduring life in the Hereafter. Allah says, "Verily, the home of the Hereafter, that is the life indeed, if they but knew" (29:64).

It is not simply the individual who benefits from Islam. Society as a whole benefits—indeed, all of humanity benefits from the teaching of Islam. Again, Allah says about the Prophet Muhammad, "And We have not sent you (O Muhammad) except as a mercy for the world" (21:107). The teachings of Islam bring about truth and justice for the entire community, allowing all members to live in a community of love, harmony and compassion.[2]

---

[1] See ibn al-Qayyim, *al-Waabil al-Sayyib*, pp. 73.

[2] It is beyond the scope of this work to discuss Islam's influence on the world in detail, the interest reader may consult Abul Hasan Ali Nadwi, *Islam and the World* (International Islamic Federation of Student Organizations, 1983).

The Ritual Acts of Worship in Islam
The purpose, goal and scope of worship

As noted earlier, the Islamic term for worship implies "servitude" to the Lord. As also discussed earlier, to worship God is actually the only goal for which all of humankind has been created. Indeed, the noblest and greatest that anyone could ever be is being a true servant and worshipper of God.

Al-Miqreezee notes that the proper form of worship entails four aspects:

(1) Determining what Allah and His Messenger (peace and blessings of Allah be upon him) love and are pleased with;

(2) The embodying and enacting of those beloved aspects in one's own heart;

(3) Enacting those aspects in one's speech;

(4) Further enacting those aspects in one's actions.[1]

Each one of these aspects is necessary if a person desires to fulfill his goal of being a true worshipper and servant of Allah. The individual first recognizes that the manner that he is to worship Allah is not based on his own individual inclinations, logic or whims. Instead, it must be based on what comes from Allah Himself. Allah is the only one who can state how He is to be worshipped. Hence, the first step is to determine what Allah wants from the individual and what is pleasing to Him. This is achieved by getting knowledge of the Quran and Sunnah. This knowledge must then be transformed into an acceptance and desire for those things in one's heart. One must recognize those things as the true good things and one, hence, must have a feeling of love for those things in one's heart. When this is accomplished, the proclamation of one's acceptance and belief as well as the application of this acceptance via one's deeds should automatically accompany it.

---

[1] Quoted from Al-Maqreezi, *Tajreed al-Tauheed al-Mufeed* by the translator of Ahmad ibn Taimiyyah, *Ibn Taymiyyah's Essay on Servitude* (Birmingham, United Kingdom: al-Hidaayah Publishing and Distribution, 1999), p. 29, fn. 54.

In general, these four aspects are usually summarized in two very important points. For anyone's worship to be proper it must be (1) performed sincerely and purely for the sake of Allah and it must be (2) in accordance with what Allah has revealed in the Quran and Sunnah.

Another very important aspect to keep in mind is that "worship" is not restricted to the ritual acts of worship or acts that one may consider "religious" or "spiritual." As noted earlier, the goal is to become as complete a servant of Allah as one can. The correct concept of servitude is very comprehensive. "Worship" or *ibaadah* is, as ibn Taimiyyah stated in his well-known and widely accepted definition of the term,

> a noun comprising every word or deed, internal or manifest, that Allah loves and approves. This includes prayer, zakat, fasting, pilgrimage, speaking the truth, fulfilling trusts, doing good to parents and relatives, keeping promises, enjoining good, forbidding evil, jihad against the disbelievers and hypocrites, good behavior towards neighbors, orphans, the poor, travelers, slaves and animals, prayer and supplication, remembering God and reading the Quran and so on; similarly it includes to love Allah and His Prophet (peace and blessings of Allah be upon him), to fear Him and turn to Him in repentance, to be patient in adversity and thankful in prosperity, to resign oneself to Allah's decrees, to put one's trust in His help, to hope for His mercy, and to fear His punishment. All of these form part of *ibaadah* (worship and servitude) to God.[1]

Hence, worship permeates every part of a person. It touches upon his internal characteristics as well as his outward actions.

In sum, worship is inclusive of:

---

[1] Ibn Taimiyyah, *Majmoo*, vol. 10, p. 449.

(a) One's relationship with the Lord,

(b) One's relationship with his own soul and its rights upon him,

(c) One's relationship with society as a whole,

(d) One's relationship with one's relatives, spouse, children and others who have special rights upon a person,

(e) One's relationship with the animals that Allah has placed in this creation,

(f) One's relationship with the environment and all the resources that Allah has created which are supposed to be used in a responsible and ethical manner.

Allah, though, did not leave humans clueless as to how they are going to be able to grow, persevere and continue in these acts of worship. Instead, Allah ordained for humans specific ritual acts of worship. These deeds are acts of worship in and of themselves but they are also acts that aid the individual in continuing along the path of worshipping Allah alone. The most important of these acts are what is known as the "five pillars of Islam." As quoted earlier, the Prophet (peace and blessings of Allah be upon him) stated, "Islam is built upon five [pillars]: testifying that there is none worthy of worship except Allah and that Muhammad is the Messenger of Allah, establishing the prayers, giving the zakat, making the pilgrimage to the House and fasting the month of Ramadhaan."[1]

A brief discussion of the four ritual pillars, as well as the important concept of supplication, follows.

Supplications and Words of Remembrance

An important act that makes the bond between the individual and Allah strong is the act of supplicating or praying[2] to Allah. These supplications may be done at any time and under any and all circumstances. They are to be done directly between the individual and Allah, with no intermediaries ever between the two.

---

[1] Recorded by al-Bukhari and Muslim.

[2] This is known as *duaa* and is distinct from the ritual prayers that form one of the pillars of Islam.

Supplicating, in itself, is an act of worship of Allah. When a person prays or supplicates to another, he is showing his trust and reliance in that other. He is demonstrating his need for the one he is praying to. He is demonstrating his trust in that person or being's ability to know, understand and fulfill his need. This kind of feeling in the heart that is reflected in supplication must be directed towards Allah only. When supplicating, the individual turns to Allah and, in so doing, he is admitting his own weaknesses while affirming Allah's ability to respond to His call and Allah's ability to fulfill His own will. In fact, the Prophet said, "Supplication is the [essence of] worship."[1] Indeed, supplicating is beloved to Allah. The Prophet (peace and blessings of Allah be upon him) said, "Whoever does not ask of Allah, He is angry with him."[2]

Hence, nothing but good should be expected from supplicating to Allah. The Messenger of Allah (peace and blessings of Allah be upon him) said, "There is no Muslim who supplicates Allah with a supplication that does not contain anything sinful or asks for the ties of kinship to be broken save that Allah gives him one of three things: either He will give him what he asks for soon, or He will delay it for him for the Hereafter or He will keep a similar evil away from him."[3]

In fact, the true believer is always desiring of having Allah's guidance at all times, never having to rely on himself. Thus, a Muslim is always in direct and constant interaction with Allah, his beloved and his Lord.

---

[1] Recorded by Ahmad, al-Nasaa`ee, Abu Dawood, al-Tirmidhi and others. According to al-Albaani, it is *sahih*. See al-Albaani, *Saheeh al-Jaami*, vol. 1, p. 641. From this, one can see how Muslims consider supplicating to anyone other than Allah is a form of associating partners with Allah and is completely prohibited. This would include praying to the prophets, not to speak of "saints" that people establish for themselves.

[2] Recorded by al-Tirmidhi. According to al-Albaani, it is *hasan*. Cf., al-Albaani, *Saheeh Sunan al-Tirmidhi*, vol. 3, p. 138.

[3] Recorded by Ahmad, Abu Yala, al-Haakim and others.

The Prayers

The importance of the prayers lies in the fact that no matter what actions one performs in his life, the most important aspect is one's relationship to Allah, that is, one's faith, God-consciousness, sincerity and worship of Allah. This relationship with Allah is both demonstrated and put into practice, as well as improved and increased, by the prayer. Therefore, if the prayers are sound and proper, the rest of the deeds will be sound and proper; and if the prayers are not sound and proper, then the rest of the deeds will not be sound and proper, as the Prophet (peace be upon him) himself stated.

In reality, if the prayer is performed properly— with true remembrance of Allah and turning to Him for forgiveness— it will have a lasting effect on the person. After he finishes the prayer, his heart will be filled with the remembrance of Allah. He will be fearful as well as hopeful of Allah. After that experience, he will not want to move from that lofty position to one wherein he disobeys Allah. Allah has mentioned this aspect of the prayer when He has said, "Verily, the prayer keeps one from the great sins and evil deeds" (29:45). Nadwi has described this effect in the following eloquent way,

> Its aim is to generate within the subliminal self of man such spiritual power, light of faith and awareness of God as can enable him to strive successfully against all kinds of evils and temptations and remain steadfast at times of trial and adversity and protect himself against the weaknesses of the flesh and the mischief of immoderate appetites.[1]

The prayer is a source of strength for the believers, as they turn towards the one and only true source of strength in the entire creation. The prayer thereby purifies the soul of many diseases, such as despair and cowardice. This powerful effect of the prayer is

---

[1] Abul Hasan Ali Nadwi, *The Four Pillars of Islam* (Lucknow, India: Academy of Islamic Research and Publications, 1976), p. 24.

alluded to in the verses, "And seek help in patience and the prayer and truly it is extremely heavy and hard except for who are humble (before Allah). (They are those) who are certain that they are going to meet their Lord, and that unto Him they are going to return" (2:45-46).

Besides being a source of strength, the prayer is also a joyous occasion and a chance for the soul to rest as it journeys in this world. It is a time for the soul and mind to completely and absolutely concentrate on the one matter that it knows is the only matter of extreme importance: its relationship with and proper worship of Allah. The soul realizes that in the act of prayer (when performed properly), the person is doing nothing other than getting closer to Allah and partially fulfilling the only purpose for which he was created. Hence, the Prophet (peace and blessings of Allah be upon him) used to tell Bilaal, "O Bilaal, make the call to the prayer and give us rest by it."[1]

When the person does slip and commits acts of filth and sin, the prayer can also purify the soul from those sins. In other words, it has a cleansing effect on the soul. Everyone is bound to make mistakes and commit sins. But these sins need not remain forever on the soul, causing it harm. Instead, there are means to remove them. One of the most important of those means is the performance of good deeds and, in particular, the prayers.

These are just some of the matters that point to the greatness and importance of the prayer. They are actually just the tip of the iceberg. The one who prays will feel for himself many other beneficial emotions that cannot be adequately captured in words.[2]

---

[1] Recorded by Ahmad and Abu Dawood. According to al-Albaani, it is *sahih*. See al-Albaani, *Saheeh al-Jaami*, vol. 2, p. 1307.

[2] For more details, see the author's *Purification of the Soul*, pp. 214-223. Much of this chapter is derived from that work. More details on the remaining pillars of Islam are found on pp. 223-266.

The Zakat

The concept of being obliged to give up a portion of one's wealth for the sake of God as an act of worship of God is something that one finds in the message of the previous prophets.[1] Its important place in the purification of the soul is touched upon by Sulaiman Nadwi who wrote,

> The main cause of spiritual illnesses of human beings is the absence of hope and fear of Allah and lack of love and attachment to Him. Cure to these illnesses is Salat [prayer]. There is also another cause of these illnesses, namely, attachment to worldly possessions, riches and wealth, instead of attachment to Allah. Zakat is the remedy for this second cause of illness.[2]

Zakat is also a strong reminder that wealth is a blessing from Allah. A wealthy person sees around him and throughout the world the kind of misery and destitution that, if Allah willed, he himself could be experiencing. This should develop a very strong feeling of humility and gratitude toward Allah.

Indeed, the believer should be actively seeking means by which he can thank Allah for the bounties Allah has given him. This feeling should drive him to perform more and more good deeds. The beautiful paradox of this is that if the zakat has this effect on him and he grows more thankful to Allah, Allah will in turn give him more blessings in this life and in the Hereafter. Allah says, "And (remember) when your Lord proclaimed: 'If you give thanks, I will give you more (of My Blessings), but if you are thankless (i.e. disbelievers), verily! My Punishment is indeed severe'" (14:7).

This act of worship highlights a fact discussed earlier concerning the scope of worship. Worship does not deal simply with

---

[1] For details, see Sulaiman Nadwi, *Worship in Islam* (Karachi: Darul Ishaat, 1994), pp. 153-155. For a detailed comparison of what is regarded by the Jews as the Law of Moses and the zakat of Islam, see Sulaiman Nadwi, pp. 162-173.

[2] Sulaiman Nadwi, p. 179.

one's interaction with his Lord (if one can somehow compartmentalize that and remove it from all other interactions) but it also deals with one's interaction with the other believers in particular and the rest of humanity in general. Via the zakat, one directly fulfills the needs of others. The basis by which one should interact with others is, once again, the worship of Allah. One interacts with others not on some secular basis or some philosophical view of human rights. Instead, one interacts with others based on a much stronger and moving foundation: on the basis of how Allah has instructed one to interact with others. In this way, that interaction actually becomes a form of worship, pleasing to Allah and aiding in the purification of one's soul.

Zakat develops within the soul a desire to sacrifice and assist others for the sake of Allah. The true believer cultivates in his heart the joy of giving for the sake of Allah, recognizing how pleased Allah is with such a deed. It is not simply a matter of removing the disease of selfishness, the ill amassing of wealth and the harms of egotism from one's heart. It is more than that. It is the replacement of those possible ill feelings with the feeling that a believer should sacrifice and work for others as a means of getting closer to Allah. This positive feeling should be so strong that even the one who has nothing or very little will want to sacrifice and give to get closer to Allah. Allah describes such believers when He said, "They give them preference over themselves, even though they were in need. And whosoever is saved from his own covetousness, such are they who will be the successful" (59:9). Hence, the feeling of not just thinking about oneself but of going out and doing good for others as an act of worship of Allah is embedded in the heart and soul of the true believer.

Zakat obviously has a very important role to play for society as a whole. There are some obvious factors that may be stated here. For example, zakat helps the poor of society as they receive wealth that they need. This should also help to strengthen the ties of brotherhood within a Muslim society, as the poor know that the rich will come to their aid through zakat and other means of charity. Even for those who are not very rich, it makes them realize that they can afford to give for the sake of Allah. They may realize that they will not starve or die if they give some of their wealth for the sake of Allah. Furthermore, it can make those who possess wealth realize that such wealth has actually come as a blessing from Allah. Hence, the person must use it in the way that is pleasing to Allah.

Fasting

Fasting is the one act of worship wherein the believer gives up his most basic needs and urges for a lengthy period of time as a form of worship of Allah. In this sense, it is definitely unique and the effects of this practice have been tied directly to the increase of God-consciousness and fear of Allah.

An important conclusion that one gets from the institution of the fast is that the natural inclinations of man—the need for food, drink and sexual intercourse, for example—are not in themselves evil. As was noted earlier, the teachings of Islam are completely consistent with the nature that Allah Himself has given mankind. Hence, these natural wants and desires are not frustrated completely nor denied outright. That would not be practical or achievable given the nature of mankind (and the ascetics throughout history, with their numerous aberrations, have actually demonstrated that fact). At the same time, though, these natural desires cannot be left to run free, as otherwise people will be indulging in their desires regardless of the negative consequences for themselves or for others (as can be witnessed in the world today with its widespread promiscuity, sexually transmitted diseases, alcohol abuse, drug abuse and so forth). These natural desires are to be harnessed—harnessed in such a way that positive results flow for the soul and even for humanity at large.

Patience or perseverance is one of the most important and healthiest qualities a person can possess and is an important quality found in the purified soul. There is a definite and clear relationship between fasting and patience. Fasting not only strengthens one's quality of patience, it actually touches upon all of the branches of patience. Patience is of three types: persevering with respect to continually performing the acts of worship, persevering with respect to refraining from what Allah has prohibited and remaining under control during times of hardship and difficulties. All three of these types are being tested and strengthened through the practice of fasting. While fasting, one adheres to what Allah has obligated, refrains from what he has forbidden of food and drink and also remains patient in the face of the hunger and thirst that he is experiencing.[1]

Fasting is an experience wherein the person leaves his wants and desires for the sake of putting what Allah wants first. This reminds him of his true goal and purpose in life. This experience allows him to put matters into proper perspective concerning what he wants out of this life and what is of true importance to him.

The Messenger of Allah (peace and blessings of Allah be upon him) once said, "Look at those who are lower than you [having less than you] and do not look at those who are above you [having more than you] as otherwise the bounties of Allah upon you would become insignificant to you."[2] In this hadith, the Prophet (peace and blessings of Allah be upon him) has given an instruction that will help one appreciate the numerous benefits that he has received from Allah. The institution of fasting can take the person even further. While fasting, the person does not just view the plight of others, but he can actually begin to feel their plight. Hence, the rich can reflect on what they have been given and give true thanks. Especially in this day and age and in some materially advanced countries, one becomes very much accustomed to easy access to food, drink, clean water, electricity and so on. Since these are readily available, the person starts to take them for granted and does not realize what a great

---

[1] Cf., Abdul Rahmaan ibn Rajab, *Lataaif al-Maarif feema al-Miwaasim al-Aam min al-Wadhaaif* (Damascus: Daar ibn Katheer, 1996), p. 284.
[2] Recorded by Muslim.

blessing they are and how so many in today's world are actually deprived of these basic needs.

At the end of a third successive verse about the fast, Allah states, "So that perhaps you will be grateful" (2:185). Thankfulness and gratitude towards Allah is an essential characteristic of the true believers.[1] People can speak about this matter in theoretical terms but there is no substitute for truly feeling the thirst, hunger and exhaustion that others have to go through on a daily basis. The Messenger of Allah (peace and blessings of Allah be upon him) was the most generous of people and he was even more generous during the fasting month of Ramadhaan.

The Pilgrimage to Mecca (The *Hajj*)

Another of the pillars and essential obligatory practices of Islam is the pilgrimage or Hajj to the House of Allah (Kabah) in Mecca. It is a very comprehensive and potentially very moving rite.

One practical aspect that occurs from the Hajj and that anyone who has performed the Hajj can testify to is that during the Hajj one can see the willingness of other humans to sacrifice for the sake of Allah. While circumambulating the Kabah, one sees people with no legs or unusable legs pulling themselves around the Kabah. One can feel the poverty of some of the fellow pilgrims and realize how much and how long they must have sacrificed and saved to make this one Hajj for the sake of Allah. This definitely moves a person and makes him reflect upon his own sacrifices for the sake of Allah. It makes him wonder whether he himself would be willing to make such great sacrifices for the sake of Allah if or when needed.

The pilgrimage requires a great deal of sacrifice on the part of the Muslim, such as the sacrifice of time, money and effort. Every believer must realize the relationship between his faith and sacrifice. Sacrifice is an essential aspect of this religion. A true believer should

---

[1] In fact, true believers are not simply grateful toward Allah but they are also grateful toward those who do them good in this world. The Messenger of Allah (peace and blessings of Allah be upon him) stated, "Whoever does not show gratitude to the people does not show gratitude to Allah." Recorded by Ahmad and al-Tirmidhi.

be willing to sacrifice one's time, wealth and even life for the sake of Allah. In addition, the true believer must sacrifice all desires and pleasures that are not consistent with the Quran and Sunnah. In fact, a true believer must sacrifice anything that comes between him and the true worship of Allah alone.

Selfishness, arrogance, looking down upon others and greed are some of the dangerous diseases that despoil the soul. One must work valiantly to remove any remnants of these diseases. The Hajj should be a helpful step in this process. This is fulfilled via a number of means:

First, in most cases, the Hajj requires a great deal of expenditures (travel, purchasing the animal to be sacrificed and so forth). These are all eagerly spent for the sake of Allah. This helps in purifying the soul from selfishness and greed. It allows the soul to experience the joy of spending some of his wealth directly for the sake of Allah.

Second, as all of the pilgrims gather at one place, in one dress, all submitting to and calling upon their one Lord for forgiveness for the multitude of sins that people commit in this world, the feeling of brotherhood and love should fill the heart of the believer. He should realize that he himself and all the Muslims all only have one purpose in life, are all marching toward one end and they are all the servants of Allah and Allah alone. There is no room for pride and arrogance here. The reality sets in that the only ways by which these different Muslims differ is in their sincerity to Allah and their good deeds. Otherwise, there is no preference nor distinction given to anyone based on nationality, race, wealth or standing in society.

All of the events that one performs at the Hajj and the historical and spiritual significance of the place in which the person performs them—a place where Adam laid the foundation for the first house of worship, a place where Abraham rebuilt that house, leaving his family alone there and a place where the Prophet Muhammad (peace and blessings of Allah be upon him) and his Companions lived the early history of Islam—should have a profound effect on the believer. He should view his own life in the light of the lives of the prophets. He should recognize his own shortcomings and the insignificance of the other aspects of this world that he gives preference to. This should drive the person to repent and ask for forgiveness from his Lord. Indeed, the feelings that should be boiling in his heart at such a place may be those which make his supplications so sincere that Allah will not turn down his pleas.

Scientific Miracles in the Quran and Sunnah

As noted earlier, the "miracle" of the final Prophet is unique. Since he was the last prophet, with no prophet coming later, his miracle has to have a lasting affect until the Day of Judgment. Such is the case with the Quran. The Quran is miraculous in many ways. However, in the past century or so, many have noted that it is miraculous in the manner in which it is perfectly consistent with scientific fact. In fact, as new discoveries are being made, people are realizing that some of those discoveries have already been alluded to in the Quran or the Sunnah. Here are some examples of this nature:

Miracles with respect to humans

Upon reading the Quran, one aspect that catches many a reader's eye is the discussion of the creation of the human within the womb of the mother. In fact, the details and the analysis are so great that Keith Moore, Professor Emeritus of Anatomy and Cell Biology at the University of Toronto, has included them in a special edition of his textbook *The Developing Human: Clinically Oriented Embryology*.[1] Commenting on the miraculous consistency between statements in the Quran and the historical development of Embryology, Dr. Moore stated in 1981, "It has been a great pleasure for me to help clarify statements in the Qur'an about human development. It is clear to me that these statements must have come to Muhammad from God, because almost all of this knowledge was not discovered until many centuries later. This proves to me that Muhammad must have been a messenger of God."[2]

---

[1] See Keith L. Moore [along with Abdul-Majeed Azzindani], *The Developing Human: Clinically Oriented Embryology [with Islamic Additions: Correlation Studies with Quran and Hadith]* Jeddah, Saudi Arabia: Dar al-Qiblah for Islamic Literature, 1983, in conjunction with W. B. Saunders Company. This is an interesting work that is comprised of Moore's complete textbook with insertions describing the same topic from the point of view of the Quran and hadith. The consistency between the two is obvious and, given the historical development of the science, amazing, given that the Quran was revealed over 1400 years ago.

[2] Quoted in I. A. Ibrahim, *A Brief Illustrated Guide to Understanding Islam* (Houston: Darussalam, 1997), p. 10. This work, in its entirety, is available at www.islam-guide.com. Ibrahim reviews and summarizes the conclusions of Moore and a number of others.

For the sake of brevity, though, it will be possible to discuss only one verse in some detail here.[1] Allah says in the Quran, "We created man from an extract of clay. Then We made him as a drop in a place of settlement, firmly fixed. Then We made the drop into an *alaqah* (leech, suspended thing, and blood clot), then We made the *alaqah* into *mudghah* (chewed-like substance)..." (23:12-14).

This brief passage is outstanding in its precise description of the actual process as well as its freedom from all of the incorrect theories and views that were prevalent at the time of Muhammad (peace and blessings of Allah be upon him). As noted in the translation, the Arabic word *alaqah* can imply leech, suspended thing or blood clot. In reality, all of these terms are descriptive of the embryo. In fact, in its earliest stage, the embryo not only actually physically looks like a leech[2] but it "obtains nourishment from the blood of the mother, similar to the leech, which feeds on the blood of others."[3] *Alaqah*, again, can also mean, "suspended thing," which is also true of the embryo in this stage as it sits hanging in the womb of the mother.[4] Finally, *alaqah* can also mean blood clot. Again, the relationship to the actual physical process is miraculous. Ibrahim writes,

> We find that the external appearance of the embryo
> and its sacs during the *alaqah* stage is similar to
> that of a blood clot. This is due to the presence of
> relatively large amounts of blood present in the
> embryo during this stage... Also, during this stage,
> the blood in the embryo does not circulate until the

---

[1] For more details concerning the different stages of human development, the interested reader may also consult Keith L. Moore, Abdul-Majeed A. Zindani and Mustafa A. Ahmed, *Quran and Modern Science: Correlation Studies* (Bridgeview, IL: Islamic Academy for Scientific Research, 1990), pp. 15-47.

[2] See I. A. Ibrahim, p. 7, Figure 1.

[3] I. A. Ibrahim, p. 6.

[4] See I. A. Ibrahim, p. 7, Figure 2.

end of the third week. Thus, the embryo as this stage is like a blood clot.[1]

The verse states that the next stage is that of a *mudghah* or "chewed-like substance." This is also an amazingly accurate description of the next embryonic stage. At this stage, the embryo develops somites at its back and these "somewhat resemble teethmarks in a chewed substance."[2]

The kind of information described above has only been "discovered" and seen by humans since the development of powerful microscopes. Ibrahim notes that Hamm and Leeuwenhoek were the first to observe human sperm cells, in 1677 due to the help of an improved microscope.[3] This took place some 1000 years after the time of the Prophet Muhammad (peace and blessings of Allah be upon him). As Moore has concluded, it seems somewhat inconceivable that the Prophet Muhammad (peace and blessings of Allah be upon him) could have known such details except via revelation from God.

Miracles with Respect to Animals

The Prophet (peace and blessings of Allah be upon him) stated, "If a housefly falls into a drink of yours, he should dip it all [into the drink] and then discard it, for one wing has a disease and the other has the cure."[4] One should recall that the Prophet (peace and blessings of Allah be upon him) was speaking at a time in which there was no knowledge of viruses, vaccines, anti-venoms and the like. However, he has propounded this statement as part of what had been revealed to him from God. In recent years, the accuracy and correctness of this statement has been verified in separate empirical tests. In one such experiment, when one wing of the fly was put into water, it was found that the water had become contaminated but when

---

[1] Ibrahim, p. 8.

[2] Quoted by Ibrahim, p. 8, from Moore and Persaud, *The Developing Human*, 5th ed., p. 8. Also see Ibrahim's figures on page 9.

[3] Ibrahim, pp. 8-10.

[4] Recorded by al-Bukhari.

the other wing of the fly was put into the water, the contaminant was removed.[1]

The Quranic discussion of the source of the constituents of animal milk is also quite illuminating. It is touched upon in chapter 16, verse 66. Earlier translators, basing their translations on apparent meanings of some of the words in the verse, have tended to miss exactly what is being stated in the verse. Bucaille, by studying the words closely, concludes that the verse should be translated in the following manner: "Verily, in cattle there is a lesson for you. We give you to drink of what is inside their bodies, coming from a conjunction between the contents of the intestine and the blood, a milk pure and pleasant for those who drink it."[2] After discussing the process by which milk is formed in the animal's body, Bucaille states,

> Here the initial process which sets everything else in motion is the bringing together of the contents of the intestine and blood at the level of the intestinal wall itself. This very precise concept is the result of the discoveries made in the chemistry and physiology of the digestive system. It was totally unknown at the time of the Prophet Muhammad and has been understood only in recent times. The discovery of the circulation of the blood, was made by Harvey roughly ten centuries after the Qur'anic Revelation.
>
> I consider that the existence in the Qur'an of the verse referring to these concepts can have no

---

[1] For details of such experiments, see Saalih ibn Ahmad Ridhaa, *Al-Ijaaz al-Ilmi fi al-Sunnah al-Nabawiyyah* (Riyadh, Saudi Arabia: Maktabah al-Ubaikaan, 2001) vol. 1, pp. 552-555 or Yoosuf al-Haaj Ahmad, *Mausooah al-Ijaaz al-Ilmi fi al-Quraan al-Kareem wa al-Sunnah al-Mutahharah* (Damascus, Syria: Maktabah ibn Hajar, 2003), pp. 297-298.

[2] Bucaille, pp. 195-196. He states that this translation is very close to the one given in the *Muntakab*, 1973, edited by the Supreme Council for Islamic Affairs.

human explanation on account of the period in which they were formulated.[1]

Miracles with Respect to the Origins of the Universe

Contemporary research has shown that the universe was, at one time, nothing but a cloud of "smoke," which is defined as "an opaque highly dense and hot gaseous composition."[2] New stars are still forming out of the remnants of that smoke. Allah says in the Quran, "Then He turned towards the heaven when it was smoke" (41:11). Bucaille explains the implication of this verse, demonstrating how it is completely consistent with the "smoke" that contemporary scientists are referring to,

> The statement of the existence of a gaseous mass
> with fine particles, for this is how the word 'smoke'
> (*dukan* in Arabic) is to be interpreted. Smoke is
> generally made up of a gaseous substratum, plus, in
> more or less stable suspension, fine particles that
> may belong to solid and even liquid states of matter
> at high or low temperature.[3]

But since the galaxy formed from this "smoke," contemporary science is saying that the heavens and the earth were actually all one connected entity and that from that entity, or "smoke," the heavens and earth were separated and created. This is also, once again, what one finds reference to in the Quran. Allah states, "Have not those who disbelieve known that the heavens and the earth were joined together as one united piece, then We parted them?" (21:30). Again, it is of interest to note the exact Arabic words used in this passage. Bucaille states,

> The reference to a separation process (*fatq*) of a
> primary single mass whose elements were initially
> fused together (*ratq*). It must be noted that in
> Arabic '*fatq*' is the action of breaking, diffusing,

---

[1] Bucaille, p. 197.

[2] Ibrahim, p. 14.

[3] Bucaille, p. 139.

separating, and that '*ratq*' is the action of fusing or binding together elements to make a homogenous whole.[1]

Dr. Alfred Kroner, Professor of Geology and the Chairman of the Department of Geology at the Institute of Geosciences, Johannes Gutenberg University, Mainz, Germany, made the following conclusion concerning what the Quran states about the origins of the universe:

> Thinking where Muhammad came from … I think it is almost impossible that he could have known about things like the common origin of the universe, because scientists have only found out within the last few years, with very complicated and advanced technological methods, that this is the case.[2]

Miracles with Respect to the Mountains

Allah says in the Quran, "Have We not made the earth an expanse and the mountains stakes" (78:6-7). Allah also says while calling upon humankind to reflect upon the various phenomena in creation, "[Reflect upon] the mountains, how they have been pitched (like a tent). The Earth how it was made even" (88:19-20).

In the light of modern science, these verses are quite illuminating. It has been shown that mountains have deep "roots." These roots go deep into the ground and are shaped like pegs.[3] This is, in other words, the same as Allah's description of the mountains as stakes, which could also be rendered into English as pegs.

Allah also says, "And the mountains (God) has fixed them firmly" (79:32). Yet another verse states, "And He has affixed into the earth mountains standing firm, lest it should shake with you" (16:15). Recent discoveries have shown that the mountains help to stabilize the earth's crust. This knowledge, of course, has only been

---

[1] Bucaille, p. 139.
[2] Quoted in Ibrahim, p. 14.
[3] See Ibrahim, p. 11.

the result of the modern theory of plate tectonics, which has developed only since the late 1960s.[1]

Many more examples of this nature could be given here but the author believes that the above should suffice to demonstrate the "scientific miracle" of the Quran that was revealed to the illiterate Prophet Muhammad (peace and blessings of Allah be upon him) over 1400 years ago.

---

[1] Ibrahim, p. 13. Also see Bucaille, pp. 180-182.

Statements of Unbiased Observers in the East and West

Throughout history, many unbiased observers of Islam have written testimonies concerning the beauties or excellence of Islam, the Quran and the Prophet Muhammad.[1] To this day, many who write about Islam are very positive in their appraisal of this noble religion. Some contemporary non-Muslims are actually quite active in trying to refute many of the false claims that one hears about Islam in the media.

Actually, some of the greatest thinkers and historians of the West and the East were extremely complimentary in their overall discussion of the religion of Islam.[2]

The author of *A History of the Intellectual Development of Europe*, John Draper wrote, "Four years after the death of Justinian, A.D. 569, was born at Mecca, in Arabia, the man who, of all men, has exercised the greatest influence upon the human race."[3] More recently, Michael H. Hart's *The 100: A Ranking of the Most Influential Persons in History* put the Prophet Muhammad number one among all the world's influential leaders.

The early American writer Washington Irving wrote a book about the Prophet Muhammad, entitled *Mahomet and His Successors*. In this work, he gives a very glowing and praising description of the Prophet. For example, he writes, "His intellectual qualities were undoubtedly of an extraordinary kind... He indulged in no magnificence of apparel, the ostentation of a petty mind... In his private dealings he was just. He treated friends and strangers, the poor and rich, the powerful and the weak, with equity, and he was

---

[1] Among non-Muslims, one can find those who vehemently attack Islam and others who show some appreciation and respect for the religion. Although this is not the place to enter into a detailed discussion of this topic, it could be demonstrated that many, perhaps the majority, of those who attack Islam are basing their attacks on false reports or notions of Islam. There are others, though, who attack Islam simply because the way of life they believe in is completely opposed to Islam and, therefore, they hold a negative, biased view of Islam.

[2] For many more quotes from numerous non-Muslim intellectuals, see *Islam—The First & Final Religion* (Karachi, Pakistan: Begum Aisha Bawany Waqf, 1978), pp. 37-93.

[3] Quoted in *Islam—The First and Final Religion*, p. 39.

beloved by the common people… His military triumphs awakened no pride nor vain glory, as they would have done had they been effected for selfish purposes…"[1]

> Lamartine, the French intellectual, wrote,

> If greatness of purpose, smallness of means, and astounding results are the three criteria of human genius, who could dare to compare any great man in modern history with Muhammad? The most famous men created arms, laws and empires only. They founded, if anything at all, no more than material powers which often crumbled away before their eyes. This man moved not only armies, legislations, empires, peoples and dynasties, but millions of men in one-third of the then inhabited world; and more than that, he moved the altars, the gods, the religions, the ideas, the beliefs and souls. On the basis of a Book, every letter of which has become law, he created a spiritual nationality which blended together peoples of every tongue and of every race…[2]

> Professor Nathaniel Schmidt wrote,

> The essential sincerity of Muhammad's nature cannot be questioned; and an historical criticism that blinks no fact, yields nothing to credulity, weighs every testimony, has no partisan interest, and seeks only the truth, must acknowledge his claim to belong to that order of prophets…[3]

One can find similar important glowing statements from noted historians and intellectuals such as Edward Gibbon, Arnold Toynbee,

---

[1] Quoted in *Islam—The First and Final Religion*, p. 46.

[2] Quoted in *Islam—The First and Final Religion*, p. 47.

[3] Quoted in *Islam—The First and Final Religion*, p. 52.

H. G. Wells, George Bernard Shaw, Will Durant, Marshall Hodgson and others.[1]

Besides historians and thinkers, even dignitaries of other faiths have stated their respect and admiration for the Prophet Muhammad. The Rev. Montgomery Watt honestly proclaimed, "To suppose Muhammad an imposter raises more problems than it solves. Moreover, none of the great figures of history is so poorly appreciated in the West as Muhammad."[2] The Hindu leader Mahatma Gandhi said about the Prophet,

> I wanted to know the best of the life of one who holds today undisputed sway over the hearts of millions of mankind... I became more than ever convinced that it was not the sword that won a place for Islam in those days in the scheme of life. It was the rigid simplicity, the utter self-effacement of the Prophet, the scrupulous regard for pledges, his intense devotion to his friends and followers, his intrepidity, his fearlessness, his absolute trust in God and in his own mission. These and not the sword carried everything before them and surmounted every obstacle... When I closed the second volume [of the Prophet's Biography], I was sorry there was not more for me to read of that great life.[3]

In recent decades, many scientists, in particular, have marveled at the miraculous nature of the Quran and have concluded that it is inconceivable that such a work could have been produced by a human some 1400 years ago.[4] For example, the French medical

---

[1] See, for example, *Islam—The First and Final Religion*, pp. 44-45, 57-58, 66-67, 73-76 and 93.

[2] Quoted in *Islam—The First and Final Religion*, p. 53.

[3] Quoted in *Islam—The First and Final Religion*, p. 44.

[4] A number of quotes from today's leading scientists in various fields of science may be found in Ibrahim, pp. 27-31.

doctor Maurice Baucaille, at the end of a comprehensive study on the Bible, the Quran and Science, wrote,

> In view of the level of knowledge in Muhammad's day, it is inconceivable that many of the statements in the Qur'an which are connected with science could have been the work of a man. It is, moreover, perfectly legitimate, not only to regard the Qur'an as the expression of a Revelation, but also to award it a very special place, on account of the guarantee of authenticity it provides and the presence in it of scientific statements which, when studied today, appear as a challenge to explanation in human terms.[1]

Dr. T. V. N. Persaud, a specialist in Anatomy, Obstetrics and related fields and a Professor at the University of Manitoba, stated, "You have someone illiterate [meaning the Prophet Muhammad] making profound pronouncements and statements that are amazingly accurate about scientific nature. I personally can't see how this could be a mere chance. There are too many accuracies and, like Dr. Moore, I have no difficulty in my mind that this is a divine inspiration or revelation which led him to these statements."[2]

Prof. Tejatat Tejasen of Chiang Mai University in Thailand stated,

> During the last three years, I became interested in the Quran... From my study... I believe that everything that has been recorded in the Quran fourteen hundred years ago must be the truth, that can be proved by scientific means. Since the Prophet Muhammad could neither read nor write, Muhammad must be a messenger who relayed this truth, which was revealed to him as an

---

[1] Maurice Bucaille, *The Bible, the Quran and Science* (Indianapolis, IN: American Trust Publications, 1978), pp. 251-252.

[2] Quoted in Ibrahim, p. 27.

enlightenment by the one who is eligible [as the] creator… Therefore, I think this is the time to say…[at this point, Prof. Tejasen makes a declaration of Islamic faith].[1]

The last personality quoted declared his faith and became a Muslim. Actually, this has been the fate of millions who have studied Islam throughout the East and the West. Some may be famous people, such as rock star Cat Stevens or German diplomat Murad Hoffman, but the vast majority are simply honest people who understand that there is some truth behind this reality and via honest and unbiased study and contemplation realize and accept the truth of Islam.

Of course, a very important question may be raised at this point: Why didn't all those who have such great things to say about Islam embrace Islam? Each individual case may be different but many may have their own personal reasons for not embracing Islam. For example, many who have grown up in the West have developed a bad taste for any form of "organized religion" and hence they see the truth but practice on their own. Others may be "happy and satisfied" with what they have and do not understand the vital necessity of moving on to the complete truth in the sight of God. Others simply do not wish to make a drastic change in their lives, even though they see the truth in something. Yet others may have social barriers to accepting such a different religion given their society or status. The reasons are various. In any case, though, Islam stands upon its own great merits. The individual should not be too concerned about what others, with their own biases and dislikes, may do or say. Instead, he should take the initiative on his own to try to search for and discover the truth. Thus, he is encouraged and invited to make his own unbiased study of Islam. As if often the case, this may lead him to the truth of Islam and a desire to then embrace Allah's religion.

This, then, leads to the final topic: How does one become a Muslim.

---

[1] Quoted in Ibrahim, p. 31.

How Does One Become a Muslim

The process by which one becomes a Muslim is quite simple and straightforward. All it entails is the declaration of one's belief. Thus, one states in front of witnesses, "I bear witness that there is none worthy of worship except Allah and I bear witness that Muhammad is the Messenger of Allah." Upon stating those sentences, one enters into the beautiful brotherhood of Islam, a brotherhood that stretches from the time of Adam until the last days of this earth.

It is recommended that one do a complete washing of one's body, such as a shower, before making this declaration. This symbolic act represents the washing away of all previous acts as one is now entering a new stage in life. The Prophet (peace and blessings of Allah be upon him) stated, "Islam wipes away whatever [sins] preceded it."[1] In other words, whether one had defiantly disobeyed God or was simply ignorant of faith, all of that is now behind the individual. He now has a new life. He should realize, though, that he has now taken his first step. There are many other wonderful steps ahead of him. He should now be prepared to grow and blossom as a devoted worshipper and servant of Allah until he finally meets Allah on the Day of Judgment, being pleased with being Allah's servant and Allah being pleased with him as His servant.

It was noted earlier that Islam is definitely a complete way of life. Upon embracing Islam, one must have the intention to submit to Allah. This means that many changes may take place in a person's life. Hence, again, it is truly a life-transforming step in many ways. One should make the commitment with that knowledge and with the firm conviction that pleasing Allah is the ultimate goal in one's life.

However, one never has to be alone in one's spiritual path. From the moment one embraces Islam, he is part of a brotherhood and sisterhood that is there for each other. In every major city throughout the world, one can find Islamic centers and mosques. It has been the experience of this author that those centers are always

---

[1] Recorded by Ahmad.

more than happy to welcome any newcomer into the fold and to try to help him or her grow as a Muslim.

By Allah's grace, He has made His religion open to everyone. There are no restrictions—all that is needed is a sincere heart willing to submit to and worship Allah alone.

May Allah guide all the sincere truthseekers to the wonderful and beautiful path of His religion, Islam.

Conclusion

This author has attempted to shed some light on the religion of Allah, Islam. This is obviously an ominous task and difficult to perform in a small number of words. Sometimes, it is difficult to put into words the beauty that one experiences. However, the author hopes that some of what has been written here has touched the heart and the mind of the reader. The only advice that this author is left to give is to encourage every reader to turn to God with a sincere heart and ask Him for guidance. Allah willing, that sincere prayer will lead the individual directly to the truth and the beauty of Islam. Amen.

Selected References

The following are some of the references used for this work. Only the references that meet the following two criteria have been reproduced here: (1) The reference is in English and (2) the reference is relevant for further study about Islam. All other references have been relegated to their respective footnotes.

Abdul Mohsen, Abdul Radhi Muhammad. *Muhammad's Prophethood: Reality or Hoax*. Riyadh, Saudi Arabia: International Islamic Publishing House. 1999.

Al-Ashqar, Umar. *Belief in Allah in the Light of the Quran and Sunnah*. Riyadh: International Islamic Publishing House. 2000.

al-Ashqar, Umar. *The World of the Jinn and Devils*. Boulder, CO: Al-Basheer Company for Publications and Translations. 1998.

Al-Azami, M. M. *The History of the Quranic Text from Revelation to Compilation: A Comparative Study with the Old and New Testaments*. Leicester, United Kingdom: UK Islamic Academy. 2003.

al-Hageel, Sulieman. *Human Rights in Islam and a Refutation of the Misconceived Allegations Associated with These Rights*. Supreme Council for Islamic Affairs. 2001.

Al-Hilali, Muhammad and Muhammad Muhsin Khan, trans. *The Noble Quran: English Translation of the Meanings and Commentary*. Madinah, Saudi Arabia: King Fahd Complex for the Printing of the Holy Quran. n.d.

Badawi, Jamal. *Muhammad in the Bible*. Halifax, Canada: Islamic Information Foundation. n.d.

Commentary on the Creed of at-Tahawi by ibn Abi al-Izz. Muhammad Abdul-Haqq Ansari, trans. Riyadh: Ministry of Higher Education. 2000.

Daniel, Norman. *Islam and the West: The Making of an Image*. Oxford, England: Oneworld Publications. 1993.

Dialogue Between Islam and Christianity: Discussion of Religious Dogma Between Intellectuals from the Two Religions. Fairfax, VA: Institute of Islamic and Arabic Sciences in America. 1999.

Dirks, Jerald F. *The Cross & the Crescent.* Beltsville, MD: Amana Publications. 2001.

Draz, Muhammad Abdullah. *The Quran: An Eternal Challenge.* Leicester, United Kingdom: The Islamic Foundation. 2001.

ibn Abdullah, Misha'al. *What Did Jesus REALLY Say?* Ann Arbor, MI: Islamic Assembly of North America. 2001.

ibn Taimiyyah, Ahmad. *Ibn Taymiyyah's Essay on Servitude.* Birmingham, United Kingdom: al-Hidaayah Publishing and Distribution. 1999.

Ibrahim, I. A. *A Brief Illustrated Guide to Understanding Islam.* Houston: Darussalam. 1997.

Idris, Jaafar Sheikh. *The Pillars of Faith.* Riyadh: Presidency of Islamic Research, Ifta and Propagation. 1984.

Islam—The First & Final Religion. Karachi, Pakistan: Begum Aisha Bawany Waqf. 1978.

Janabi, T.H. *Clinging to a Myth: The Story Behind Evolution.* Burr Ridge, IL: American Trust Publications. 2001.

Khan, Muhammad Muhsintrans. *Sahih al-Bukhari.* Riyadh, Saudi Arabia: Darussalam Publishers and Distributors. 1997.

Maqsood, Ruqaiyyah Waris. *Thinking About God.* Plainfield, IN: American Trust Publications. 1994.

Nadwi, Abul Hasan Ali. *Islam and the World.* International Islamic Federation of Student Organizations. 1983.

Nadwi, Abul Hasan Ali. *The Four Pillars of Islam.* Lucknow, India: Academy of Islamic Research and Publications. 1976.

Njozi, Hamza Mustafa. *The Sources of the Quran: A Critical Review of the Authorship Theories.* Riyadh, Saudi Arabia: World Assembly of Muslim Youth. 1991.

Philips, Bilal. *The Fundamentals of* Tawheed *(Islamic Monotheism).* Birmingham, United Kingdom: Al-Hidaayah Publishing and Distribution.

Philips, Bilal. *The Purpose of Creation.* Sharjah, UAE: Dar al Fatah. 1995.

Pickthall, Muhammad Marmaduke, trans. *The Glorious Quran* New York: Muslim World League. n.d.

Qutb, Sayyed. *Islam and Universal Peace.* Indianapolis, IN: American Trust Publications. 1977.

Reeves, Minou. *Muhammad in Europe: A Thousand Years of Western Myth-Making.* Washington Square, New York: New York University Press. 2000.

Saheeh International. *The Quran: Arabic Text with Corresponding English Meaning.* London: AbulQasim Publishing House. 1997.

Siddiqi, Abdul Hamid, trans. *Sahih Muslim.* Lahore, Pakistan: Sh. Muhammad Ashraf Publishers & Booksellers. n.d.

Tabbarah, Affif A. *The Spirit of Islam: Doctrine & Teachings.* Hasan T. Shoucair, trans. 2nd Edition revised by Rohi Baalbaki. 1988.

Zarabozo, Jamaal al-Din. *Purification of the Soul: Concept, Process and Means.* Denver, CO: Al-Basheer Publications and Translations. 2002.

Table of Contents

www.ingramcontent.com/pod-product-compliance
Lightning Source LLC
LaVergne TN
LVHW020751200726
843506LV00009B/986

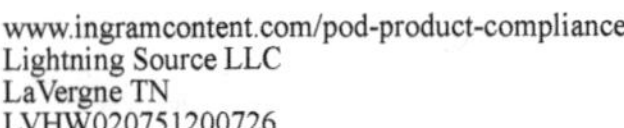